**"People For Centuries Have Been Fascinated With Glass. It's The Most Magical Of Materials."**

Dale Chihuly
From his book, *Chihuly's Baskets*

# Tying Glass Bead Flies

Joe J. Warren

Frank Amato
PORTLAND

# DEDICATION

This book is dedicated to my wife, Melissa, for her ever lasting patience and support. Also to my daughters, Yoshie, Ashley and Katy, and my parents, Jim and Josephine Warren.

**In memory of John "Ricochet" Thomas**

Admired friend and fellow angler who always lead the way in conserving and protecting our angling resource for the enjoyment of many fishing years to come.

# ACKNOWLEDGMENTS

Through the writing of this book, I have come to realize that this type of endeavor is not accomplished single-handedly. I am very grateful to numerous friends for their encouragement, support and ideas. I wish to specially acknowledge those who have had direct involvement in the planning, shaping and production of this fly-tying book: To Lee Clark for writing the "Foreword" and drawing the glass-bead fly illustrations. He has always given me the confidence to go for it, and holds me accountable for not forgetting my family while pursuing my fly-fishing interests. Alec Jackson for his splendid photography and knowledgeable insight all the way through this project. My editing advisor and close friend, Ken Tiffan, for taking the time to proofread the manuscript. Dale Chihuly and the Chihuly Studio for granting use of the Chihuly Basket photo used for the cover. Dennis Brown of Temple Fork Outfitters and Randy Babbit of Spirit River for their suggestions that helped build a foundation for this book, also for the bead samples used in the color charts and fly patterns. Bill Chase and Paul Betters of Angler Sport Group for providing Daiichi hooks and the hook plate. Bill Myers for his assistance in tying flies for the step-by-step photography. All of the fly-tiers who shared their patterns in the plates and tying steps, adding immensely to the diversity of this book: Marrisa Babbitt, Randy Babbitt, Bill Black, Dennis Brown, Phil Brummet, Chuck Cameron, John Ciulla, Lee Clark, Henry Hoffman, Joe Miltenberger, Randy Mock, Bill Myers, Jim Pettis, Rainy Riding, Ken Tiffan and Jim Schollmeyer, his talent in photographing flies never ceases to amaze, yielding photos which enhance all books he contibutes to. And finally, to my publisher, Frank Amato, for his willingness to explore a new area in fly tying.



Published in 1997 by
**Frank Amato Publications, Inc.**
PO Box 82112
Portland, Oregon 97282
(503) 653-8108

Softbound: ISBN: 1-57188-107-7 UPC: 0-66066-00301-0
Hardbound: ISBN: 1-57188-108-5 UPC: 0-66066-00302-7

Fly illustrations: Lee Clark
Fly Photography: Alec Jackson and Jim Schollmeyer
All finished flies and steps tied by Joe J. Warren unless credited otherwise.
Front cover photograph: Alec Jackson
Frontispiece photograph: Jim Schollmeyer
Title Page photograph: Joe Warren
Book design: Tony Amato

**About the Cover:** The background for the cover is a photograph of a Chihuly Basket, Sky Blue Basket Set with Cobalt Lip Wraps, 1992, sculptured by world-renown glass artist, Dale Chihuly. Dale has been sculpturing glass for more than 30 years and is highly recognized for his series of glass baskets, sea forms and Macchia (spotted) vessel sculptures.

The basket image was originally photographed by Terry Rishel for the book, *Chihuly Baskets*, 1994.

Printed in Hong Kong

3 5 7 9 10 8 6 4 2

# Table of Contents

# Foreword

I first met Joe Warren in September of 1993 during a Christian men's retreat high in the hills above Lebanon, Oregon. It wasn't long after our introduction that we began sharing our avid interests in fly fishing and fly tying. Joe mentioned he was experimenting with glass beads in fly tying. I knew about metal-type bead-head flies from my reading, but I couldn't visualize how glass beads could be used to dress a fly. I thought it was a crazy idea. In fact, I totally agreed with a friend of his who said they were fishing lures, not flies. Joe continued his justification of glass-bead flies with enthusiasm and soon my attitude changed. It wasn't a crazy idea, but a very creative fly-tying approach.

When I asked where he got the idea, Joe explained that he discovered the glass beads while browsing through the aisles of a craft store. He was visually captivated by the sparkle and sheen of the glass beads. A closer look revealed varied sizes and many colors. Immediately Joe began thinking about the tying possibilities and decided to purchase some to experiment with. His attempts led to a personal acceptance of the idea and further thought and research at the vise and on the water blossomed into this book you now hold.

Personally, I'm fascinated with Joe's use of this novel approach. I enjoy using non-traditional tying materials myself. Frito-Lay chip bag material has been incorporated into many of my fly patterns. The macramé cord I use in tying my well-known pattern, the Clark's Stonefly, was discovered in a craft store, not a fly-fishing shop. I never seem to stop looking for "found materials", an artistic term referring to non-traditional media. I guess it comes from being an artist and teacher for over thirty years.

Whether you are a beginner or advanced fly tier, this book will be of interest to you. Joe includes easy step-by-step tying instructions and many photographs showing a wide variety of uses for the glass bead.

I have tied flies for the last four decades and Joe's unique contribution to fly design has greatly influenced what I am doing at the vise today. I welcome you to Joe Warren's new approach to the art of fly tying, and hope you discover for yourself the versatility and beauty of glass-bead flies.

—Lee Clark
St. Helens, Oregon

Lee Clark, creator of the Clark's Stonefly.

# Introduction

Without the introduction of new materials, fly tying would be pretty boring, and very limited as an art. I chose to use glass beads in my fly tying because I prefer not to limit myself with traditional fly-tying materials like feathers, fur, or tinsel. For the most part I enjoy being a fly tier who focuses on fishing flies using "any" type of material that will enhance the look or movement of the fly for any fishing situation I might encounter. Perhaps one of the most gratifying aspects of tying a fly is the experimentation with a novel material to develop a new pattern or enhance an existing one. New materials provide a great stimulus to fly tying, producing the "right" fly can inspire greater enthusiasm while it is being fished.

It is interesting to note that glass beads have been used with flies as early as the 1940s, if not sooner. In *Streamer Fly Fishing In Fresh and Salt Water* (1950), by Joseph D. Bates, Jr., two shad flies are illustrated with a quarter-inch, red glass bead strung on the leader ahead of the fly. This type of fly was known as the Silver Yank Shad Fly. Orange and yellow glass beads were also used. My first experience tying flies with glass beads started in the dead of winter in 1992. Discovering the glass beads was dumb luck that transpired in a craft store. I had no business there but waiting for my wife. My seeing the glass beads was merely coincidental, and perhaps the only the reason I noticed them at all was because I have that disease known as "fly fishing on the brain". The glass beads jumped out at me as I was strolling down an aisle. There had to be hundreds of them on the display rack, and the sparkling cast gleamed more colors than a rainbow. I have always been an avid user of Flashabou and Krystal Hair, which is probably why the glass beads caught my attention in the first place. But this was a different look, the beads did not just reflect the light, they also absorbed and refracted it. These features were increasingly enhanced by the multitude of colors in various finishes, which included iridescent, silver-lined, and inside-colored beads.

Like a kid in a candy store, I carefully examined the various sizes and colors only to be further perplexed by the choices. There were at least four different sizes. I selected the larger beads for my initial experiment, speculating that surely a large bead would slide onto a hook shank. The bead slid onto the hook easily and by pinching down the hook's barb there was more leeway to fit larger size hooks. I added a yarn foundation to eliminate the bead's looseness on the hook, which also helped by aligning the beads for an even appearance. While visualizing the beads' lustrous and translucent properties, I began my first series of glass bead patterns using Pacific salmon and steelhead flies and substituting traditional body materials. The appearance was striking whether I used one or many beads on the fly. Not only did the new look make a great impression, the beads were durable enough to be fished extensively with minimal breakage.

After gaining confidence in working with large beads, I began experimenting with smaller beads on various trout patterns using smaller hooks. Glass bead trout flies including nymphs, larvae, pupae and scuds were easy to tie and were complemented with a realistic look from the translucent beads and the impression they gave of a segmented body.

The vast assortment of colors, finishes, and sizes augments a tier's ability to imitate a predator's food, whether it is an insect's translucent body or a minnow's sheen. As you flip through the following pages, you will appreciate the special effects that glass beads generate for any fly pattern, especially when considering the three most important elements of imitation: size, shape and color. In addition, the diversity of application that glass beads have to fly tying is clearly illustrated in four chapters which will guide you in tying many styles of patterns whether you fish frigid trout streams or the big blue saltwater. The patterns I have selected for the tying steps will provide a basic foundation that will enable you to duplicate other patterns, or start you in the direction of creating your own patterns.

I am privileged to have obtained contributions from 15 fly tiers whose tying techniques and patterns have made this book a complete project. As a result, a wide variety of flies are presented for virtually all types of fly fishing. I am not certain how many different species have been taken on glass-bead flies, but the list is substantial and continues to grow, including species of panfish, bass, trout, salmon, and saltwater.

I hope that you have creative moments tying with glass beads and exciting adventures fishing with your glass-bead flies. The art of tying glass-bead flies is in its infancy, I look forward to seeing the development of future fly patterns.

Joe J. Warren
Carson, Washington

# Hooks, Beads, Tools & Accessories

## Introduction to Beads

There are more uses for glass beads than just crafting jewelry. Despite their fragile reputation, glass beads are hardy enough for the fly fisher, however their durability is dependent on how well they are secured or fastened on the hook. When I began using glass beads, I determined that wrapping the hook shank with a foundation of thread, yarn, or floss, would allow the beads to sit firmly on the hook and align with each other to give a balanced appearance.

Because larger beads have bigger openings, you must fill the gap between the hook shank and the inside surface of the bead. The bead's tight fit on the hook helps absorb the shock if it impacts with an object. For example, while nymphing for trout in pocket water where protruding boulders were present, my glass bead nymph occasionally came into contact with one of these boulders. I'd inspect the fly and find that no beads were broken (bead flies delivered from a whipping back cast to a hard surface don't fare as well, but, then again, not many flies do).

Tying bead flies with materials within the beads and/or around them, are excellent ways to preserve the life of the fly. Additional tying techniques that help construct a lasting bead fly are the bead lock and the bead weave which are illustrated in Chapters 3 (Metallic P.T.) and 4 (Cranefly), respectively.

Occasionally, concern is raised regarding the fish's sensitivity or reaction to the texture of glass beads. First, fish do not possess super sonar organs to detect "foreign" materials before they come into contact with them. Generally, when a predator is searching or waiting for prey, vision is the primary sense used. Second, once the fish has committed itself to striking your fly you have accomplished your task and hopefully have enough savvy to set the hook, or luck is with you and the fish hooks itself. I hope there are no fly fishers out there expecting to have their fly swallowed into the fish's gullet! Texture is the least important factor in imitation.

The one question I most often hear is, "Where do you go to shop for beads?" Interest in using glass beads for fly tying has surged over the last year, there are currently several bead vendors ranging from craft/fabric stores and bead shops to your local fly-fishing shop. As previously mentioned, a craft store is where I made my discovery of glass beads. However, it was not as simple as threading a bunch of beads on a hook and calling it a fly. After spending numerous hours researching the bead market and fitting beads on hooks ranging from size 18 to 3/0, I discovered a noticeable amount of inconsistency in the quality of beads. Many of them were of poor quality, and unacceptable for fly tying. With many countries importing beads into the United States, it can be a real guessing game finding adequate tying beads. One problem is that the holes in some beads are too small, limiting their fit to only smaller hooks. A large bead on a small hook causes disproportion between the imitation and hook size, including a decrease in the hook's gape. Some beads have square holes which don't always fit properly on a hook, while others lack a smooth cylindrical shape.

I have collaborated closely with two fly-fishing companies, Temple Fork Outfitters, Inc. in Logan, Utah, and Spirit River, Inc., in Roseburg, Oregon, in their marketing of quality glass beads for the fly-tying industry. I was given the opportunity to scrutinize glass beads in five different sizes from both of these companies and can assure you their bead quality is impeccable. These are glass beads marketed for the specific purpose of fly tying! Whether you purchase Spirit River Hi-Lite glass beads or Temple Fork Killer Caddis glass beads, you will be completely satisfied when tying a glass-bead pattern. Because these beads are sold for fly tying and are carried in fly shops, it should be a comfort to know that someone who knows fly fishing can assist you with your questions and needs. As you embark on your own glass-bead hunt, just remember the old saying, "You get what you pay for."

## Hooks

When selecting hooks for tying glass-bead flies, quality is an important criteria. Premium hooks are designed with smooth, gradual bends, mini barbs, and blemish-free finishes and are your best choice for tying glass-bead fly patterns. In my opinion, the Japanese are the leaders in manufacturing premium hooks, companies such as Daiichi, Gamakatsu, Tiemco and Dai-Riki provide superior products. These hooks incorporate the latest technology to produce the best tempering of steel and chemically-sharpened points, both of which maximize fish-catching ability.

I prefer to tie my flies on Daiichi hooks, they are of superb quality and are the most compatible for tying with glass beads. Daiichi is unsurpassed in its large selection of hook styles and sizes. Daiichi's vast assortment in hook design is the result of requests by accomplished fly tiers, including Alec Jackson, Dick Talleur, and Darrel Martin.

Daiichi has completed their latest hook, the Dennis Brown Glass Bead Hook, designed specifically for tying beaded nymphs, scuds, larvae, or pupae. The features of this curved hook include an extension of the forward shank, no barb, an upturned eye that is closer to the point, and an offset point, all of which contribute to easier glass-bead fly tying, and better hooking and holding of fish. With any standard hook, it is always advantageous to offset the point with a pair of pliers to increase hooking potential.

You will notice that the majority of flies in this book are tied on Daiichi hooks. To identify a hook type used for a certain pattern, note the hook number in the materials list and refer to the Daiichi Hook Chart on the facing page for an exact description of that hook. For example, if a pattern lists a Daiichi 1720 hook, this equates to a standard long-bodied nymph hook, 3X-long, down-eye, 1X-strong or heavy.

# Chemically Sharpened  Needle Point Hooks

**1100**
Wide-Gape Dry Fly Hook
Model Perfect Bend, Oversized Down -Eye, 1X-Fine, Mini-Barb, Bronzed.
**Uses: Standard Dry Flies.**
**Sizes: 16, 18, 20, 22, 24**

**1110**
Wide-Gape Dry Fly Hook
Model Perfect Bend, Oversized Straight-Eye 1X-Fine, "Mini-Barb", Bronzed.
**Uses: Standard Dry Flies.**
**Sizes: 12, 14, 16, 18, 20, 22, 24, 26**

**1130**
Special Wide-Gape Hook
Continuous Bend, Down -Eye, 1X-Short, Forged, Reversed, Bronzed. **Uses: Scud, Shrimp, Grubs, Pupae, San Juan Worm.**
**Sizes: 10, 12, 14, 16, 18, 20, 22, 24**

**1140**
Special Wide-Gape Hook
Continuous Bend, Up-Eye, 1X-Fine, 1X-Short, Forged, Reversed, Bronzed.
**Uses: Midge Pupae, Micro-Caddis.**
**Sizes: 18, 20, 22**

**1150**
Heavy Wide-Gape Hook
Continuous Bend, Up-Eye, 1X-Strong, Forged, Reversed, Bronzed or Gold
**Uses: Scud, Shrimp, Grubs, Pupae, San Juan Worm.**
**Sizes: 8, 10, 12, 14, 16, 18**

**1170**
Standard Dry Fly Hook
Round Bend, Standard Shank Length, Down-Eye, Forged, Bronzed.
**Uses: Traditional Dry Fly Patterns.**
**Sizes: 8, 10, 12, 14, 16**

**1180**
Standard Dry Fly Hook, "Mini-Barb"
Round Bend, Standard Shank Length, Down-Eye, Bronzed or Crystal™ Finish
**Uses: Traditional Dry Fly Patterns.**
**Sizes: 6, 8, 10, 12, 14, 16, 18, 20, 22, 24**

**1190**
Standard Dry Fly Hook, "Barbless"
Round Bend, Standard Shank Length, Down-Eye, Bronzed.
**Uses: Traditional Dry Fly Patterns.**
**Sizes: 8, 10, 12, 14, 16, 18, 20, 22, 24**

**1220**
Darrel Martin's Dry Fly Hook
Sproat Bend, Upturned Tapered Shank, Down-Eye, Standard Wire, Forged, Mini-Barb, Slightly Offset, Bronzed or Crystal™ Finish. **Uses: Traditional Dry Flies.**
**Sizes: 14, 16, 18, 20, 22, 24**

**1250**
Dennis Brown Glass Bead Hook
Continuous Bend, Up-Eye, Standard Wire, 1x-Long, Barbless, Slightly Offset. **Uses: Killer Caddis™, Beaded Nymphs, Scuds, Shrimp, Grubs, Pupae.**
**Sizes: 12, 14, 16, 18,**

**1270**
Multi-Use Curved Hook
York Bend, Straight-Eye, 3X-Long, Forged, Bronzed.
**Uses: Hoppers and Terrestrials, Stonefly Nymphs.**
**Sizes: 4, 6, 8, 10, 12, 14, 16, 18, 20, 22**

**1273**
Curved Shank Nymph Hook, Red
York Bend, Straight-Eye, 3X-Long, 1X-Strong, Heavy Wire, Red. **Uses: Nymphs.**
**Sizes: 8, 10, 12, 14, 16, 18, 20, 22**

**1280**
2X-Long Dry Fly Hook
Round Bend, Down-Eye, 2X-Long, Fine Wire, "Mini-Barb", Bronzed.
**Sizes: 6, 8, 10, 12, 14, 16**

**1310**
Short-Shank Dry Fly Hook
Round Bend, Down-Eye, 1X-Short, Bronzed.
**Uses: Standard Dry Flies with Wide Gape, Short-Bodied Dry Flies.**
**Sizes: 8, 10, 12, 14, 16, 18, 20, 22**

**1330**
Short-Shank Dry Fly Hook, Up-Eye
Round Bend, 1X-Short, Bronzed.
**Uses: Standard Dry Flies with Wide Gape, Short-Bodied Dry Flies, Tricos, Midges.**
**Sizes: 8, 10, 12, 14, 16, 18, 20, 22, 24**

**1480**
Special Purpose Dry Fly Hook
Limerick Bend, Straight-Eye, 1X-Fine, 2X-Short, "Mini-Barb", Bronzed.
**Uses: Midges, Spiders, Variants.**
**Sizes: 12, 14, 16, 18, 20, 22, 24**

**1510**
Glo-Bug Hook
Sproat Bend, Down-Eye, 3X-Short, Bronzed.
**Uses: Egg Patterns, Spiders, Ants.**
**Sizes: 6, 8, 10, 12, 14, 16, 18**

**1530**
Heavy Wet Fly Hook, 2X-Strong
Sproat Bend, Down-Eye, 1X-Short, Bronzed.
**Uses: Short Bodied Wets, Nymphs, Steelhead Flies.**
**Sizes: 4, 6, 8, 10, 12, 14, 16**

**1550**
Standard Wet Fly Hooks
Sproat Bend, Down-Eye, Bronzed.
**Uses: Traditional Wet Flies.**
**Sizes: 2, 4, 6, 8, 10, 12, 14, 16, 18**

**1560**
Traditional Nymph Hook
Sproat Bend, Down-Eye, 1X-Strong, 1X-Long , Bronzed.
**Uses: Wet Flies, Traditional Nymph Patterns.**
**Sizes: 6, 8, 10, 12, 14, 16, 18**

**1640**
Multi-Use Dry Fly Hook
Round Bend, Straight Eye, 2X-Short, Reversed, Forged, Bronzed. **Uses: Caddisflies, Spiders, Eggs, Tricos, Extended-Body Dry Flies.**
**Sizes: 2, 4, 6, 8, 10, 12, 14, 16, 18, 20**

**1710**
Standard Nymph Hook, 2X-Long
Round Bend, Down-Eye, 1X-Strong, Forged, Bronzed. **Uses: Wet Flies, Standard Nymph Patterns, Muddlers.**
**Sizes: 2, 4, 6, 8, 10, 12, 14, 16, 18**

**1720**
Long-Bodied Nymph Hook, 3X-Long
Round Bend, Down-Eye, 1X-Strong, Forged, Bronzed. **Uses: Muddlers, Long-Bodied Nymphs, Woolly Buggers, Small Streamers.**
**Sizes: 4, 6, 8, 10, 12, 14, 16, 18**

**1730**
Bent-Shank Nymph Hook, 3X-Long
Round Bend, Down-Eye, 1X-Strong, Forged, Bronzed.
**Uses: Stonefly Nymphs, Crab Patterns.**
**Sizes: 4, 6, 8, 10, 12, 14**

**1740**
Up-Eye Nymph Hook
Round Bend, Up-Eye, 2X-Heavy, Bronzed.
**Uses: Standard Nymph Patterns.**
**Sizes: 6, 8, 10, 12, 14, 16**

**1750**
Straight-Eye Streamer Hook
4X-Long, Round Bend, 1X-Strong, Forged, Bronzed.
**Uses: Muddlers, Streamers, Zonkers, Bucktails.**
**Sizes: 4, 6, 8, 10, 12, 14**

**1770**
Swimming Nymph Hook
Sproat Bend, Straight-Eye, 1X-Fine, 3X-Long Forged, Bronzed.
**Uses: Leeches, Nymphs, San Juan Worms.**
**Sizes: 6, 8, 10, 12, 14, 16**

**1850**
Flat-Eye Streamer Hook
4X-Long, Round Bend, 1X-Strong, Forged, Bronzed.
**Uses: Free Swimming Patterns.**
**Sizes: 6, 8, 10, 12**

**1870**
Gary Borger's Larva Hook
York Bend, 3X-Long Curved Shank, Up-Eye, 2X-Heavy Wire, Bronzed.
**Uses: Swimming Nymphs and Larval Insect Patterns.**
**Sizes: 4, 6, 8, 10, 12, 14**

**2050**
Alec Jackson Spey Fly Hook
Curved Shank, Tapered Loop Up-Eye, Forged, Bronze, Black, Nickel, Gold or Blue.
**Uses: Salmon/Steelhead Flies.**
**Sizes: 3/0, 1-1/2, 3, 5, 7**

**2131**
Bob Veverka's Classic Salmon Hook
Slightly Curved Shank, Tapered Loop Up-Eye, Round Wire, Black, Gold or Blue.
**Uses: Salmon/Steelhead Flies.**
**Sizes: 2, 4, 6, 8, 10**

**2141**
Straight-Eye Salmon Hook
Improved Limerick Bend, Tapered Loop Eye, Feather Wing Streamers, Muddler Minow, Woolly Buggers, Steelhead Flies, Bone Fish Patterns, Standard, Black. **Sizes: 1, 2, 4, 6**

**2151**
Curved-Shank Salmon Hook
Tapered Loop Straight-Eye, Forged, Black Finish.
**Uses: Salmon/Steelhead Flies.**
**Sizes: 1, 2, 4, 6, 8, 10**

**2161**
Curved-Shank Salmon Hook
Tapered Loop Up-Eye, Forged, Black Finish.
**Uses: Salmon/Steelhead Flies.**
**Sizes: 1, 2, 4, 6**

**2170**
Multi-Use Wet Fly Hook
Round Bend, Straight-Eye, 1X-Short, Shank Bent-Up, Forged, Reversed, Bronzed, Green or Black.
**Uses: Eggs, Emergers, San Juan Worm.**
**Sizes: 2, 4, 6, 8, 10, 12**

**2220**
Down-Eye Streamer Hook
4X-Long, Round Bend, 1X-Strong, Forged, Bronzed. **Uses: Muddlers, Streamers, Woolly Buggers, Zonkers.**
**Sizes: 1, 2, 4, 6, 8, 10, 12, 14**

**2271**
Salmon Streamer Hook
Improved Limerick Bend, Tapered Loop Turned-Down Eye, 6X-Long, Long Shank Streamer Patterns, 1X-Heavy, Black.
**Sizes: 1, 2**

**2340**
Traditional Streamer Hook
6X-Long, Limerick Bend, Down-Eye, 1X-Strong, Bronzed.
**Uses: Classic Streamers, Bucktails.**
**Sizes: 4, 6, 8, 10, 12**

**2370**
7X-Long Streamer Hook
Modified Limerick Bend, Tapered Loop Eye, 3X-Heavy Wire, Bronzed.
**Uses: Classic Streamers.**
**Sizes: 2, 4, 6, 8, 10**
Designed by Dick Talleur

**2421**
Multi-Use Salmon/Steelhead Hook
Tapered Loop Up-Eye, Forged, Black Finish.
**Uses: Low-Water Patterns, Salmon and Steelhead Dry Flies.**
**Sizes: 2, 4, 6, 8, 10, 12**

**2441**
Traditional Salmon/Steelhead Hook
Tapered, Loop Up-Eye, 1X-Strong, Forged, Black.
**Uses: Classic Atlantic Salmon Wet Flies, Hairwing Salmon, Steelhead Flies.**
**Sizes: 2/0, 1/0, 1, 2, 4, 6, 8**

**2451**
Short Shank Salmon/Steelhead Hook
O'Shaughnessy Bend, Straight Eye, Forged, Black Finish. **Uses: Salmon/Steelhead Flies, Salmon Trailer, Bass Flies, Tube Flies.**
**Sizes: 4/0, 3/0, 2/0, 1/0, 1, 2, 4, 6, 8**

**2460**
Multi-Use Aberdeen Hook
3X-Long, Straight Eye, Black, Bronze or Nickel.
**Uses: Muddlers, Zonkers, Bucktails, Matukas, Bass Flies, Woolly Buggers.**
**Sizes: 6/0, 4/0, 3/0, 2/0, 1/0, 1, 2, 4, 6, 8, 10, 12, 14, 16, 18**

**2546**
Saltwater Fly Hook
Stainless Steel, O'Shaugnessy Bend, Straight-Eye, Forged, Ground Needle Point. **Uses: Bonefish, Tarpon, and Other Ocean Patterns. Sizes: 8/0, 6/0, 5/0, 4/0, 3/0, 2/0, 1/0, 1, 2, 4, 6**

**2571**
Boss Steelhead Hook
Sproat Bend, 3X-Short Shank, 2X-Heavy Wire, Slightly Down-Eye, Forged, Reversed, Black Finish.
**Uses: Steelhead Flies, Egg Patterns**
**Sizes: 2, 4, 6, 8**

**2720**
Wide Gape "Stinger Hook"
Light Wire, Straight-Eye, Bronzed.
**Uses: Deer Hair Bass Bugs, Divers, Frogs, Mice.**
**Sizes: 5/0, 3/0, 1/0, 2**

**4250**
Salmon Egg Hook
Up-Eye, Short Shank, Forged, Reversed, Red, Bronzed or Gold.
**Sizes: 4, 6, 8, 10, 12, 14**

**7131**
Double Salmon Hook
Limerick Bend, Up-Eye, Forged, Black Finish.
**Sizes: 4, 6, 8, 10, 12**

# X-large and Large Beads

**Color:** Crystal, pearl
**Description:** Iridescent
**Sizes:** X-large, large, medium, small, x-small

**Color:** Iridescent blue
**Description:** Iridescent
**Size:** X-large

**Color:** Iridescent purple
**Description:** Iridescent
**Size:** X-large

**Color:** Black
**Description:** Metallic
**Size:** X-large

**Color:** Gunmetal, peacock
**Description:** Metallic
**Sizes:** X-large, large, medium, small, x-small

**Color:** Creamy white
**Description:** Pearl
**Size:** X-large

**Color:** Pale pink
**Description:** Pearl
**Size:** X-large

**Color:** Bottle green
**Description:** Silver-lined
**Size:** X-large

**Color:** Diamond, clear/pearl, silver
**Description:** Silver-lined
**Sizes:** X-large, large, medium, small, x-small

**Color:** Scarlet, ruby red
**Description:** Silver-lined
**Sizes:** X-large, large, small, x-small

**Color:** Insect green
**Description:** Translucent
**Sizes:** Large, small

**Color:** Root beer
**Description:** Translucent
**Sizes:** Large, small

**Color:** Tan
**Description:** Translucent
**Size:** Large

**Color:** Black
**Description:** Opaque
**Sizes:** Large, medium, small, x-small

**Color:** Gold, gold/pearl
**Description:** Silver-lined
**Sizes:** Large, medium, small, x-small

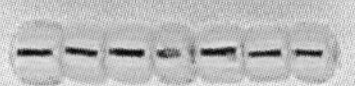
**Color:** Yellow/pearl
**Description:** Silver-lined
**Sizes:** Large, small

**Color:** Amber, orange/pearl
**Description:** Silver-lined
**Sizes:** Large, small

**Color:** Aquamarine, light blue
**Description:** Silver-lined
**Sizes:** Large, small

**Color:** Medium blue
**Description:** Silver-lined
**Sizes:** Large, small

**Color:** Dark blue
**Description:** Silver-lined
**Sizes:** Large, small

**Color:** Green/pearl
**Description:** Silver-lined
**Sizes:** Large, small

**Color:** Caddis green, olive/pearl
**Description:** Silver-lined
**Sizes:** Large, small

**Color:** Root beer, brown/pearl
**Description:** Silver-lined
**Sizes:** Large, small

# Medium, Small, and X-small Beads

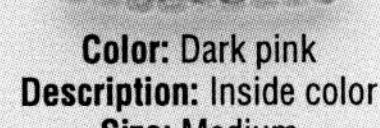

**Color:** Dark pink
**Description:** Inside color
**Size:** Medium

**Color:** Jalapeño
**Description:** Inside color
**Size:** Medium

**Color:** Ginger
**Description:** Inside color
**Size:** Medium

**Color:** Pale yellow
**Description:** Inside color
**Size:** Medium

**Color:** Iridescent plum
**Description:** Metallic
**Size:** Medium

**Color:** Charcoal
**Description:** Metallic
**Size:** Medium

**Color:** Brown
**Description:** Metallic
**Size:** Medium

**Color:** Steel
**Description:** Metallic
**Size:** Medium

**Color:** White
**Description:** Pearl
**Size:** Medium

**Color:** Chamois, sulphur
**Description:** Pearl
**Size:** Medium

**Color:** Pink
**Description:** Pearl
**Size:** Medium

**Color:** Yellow
**Description:** Translucent
**Size:** Medium

**Color:** Red
**Description:** Translucent
**Size:** Medium

**Color:** Aqua
**Description:** Translucent
**Size:** Medium

**Color:** Ice blue
**Description:** Translucent
**Size:** Medium

**Color:** Blueberry
**Description:** Translucent
**Sizes:** Medium, small

**Color:** Shrimp, rainbow pink
**Description:** Translucent
**Size:** Medium

**Color:** Dorado, rainbow green
**Description:** Translucent
**Size:** Medium

**Color:** Red
**Description:** Frost
**Size:** Small

**Color:** Chartreuse
**Description:** Inside color
**Size:** Small

**Color:** Neon yellow
**Description:** Inside color
**Size:** Small

**Color:** Golden yellow
**Description:** Inside color
**Size:** Small

**Color:** Honey Gold
**Description:** Iridescent
**Size:** Small

**Color:** Autumn
**Description:** Iridescent
**Size:** Small

**Color:** Amber
**Description:** Iridescent
**Size:** Small

**Color:** Orange
**Description:** Iridescent
**Size:** Small

**Color:** Scarlet, salmon pink
**Description:** Iridescent
**Size:** Small

**Color:** Wine
**Description:** Iridescent
**Size:** Small

**Color:** Light green
**Description:** Iridescent
**Size:** Small

**Color:** Caddis green
**Description:** Iridescent
**Size:** Small

**Color:** Silver
**Description:** Metallic
**Size:** Small

**Color:** Gold
**Description:** Metallic
**Size:** Small

**Color:** Blue dun
**Description:** Metallic
**Size:** Small

**Color:** Black shadow
**Description:** Metallic
**Sizes:** Small, X-small

**Color:** Gray
**Description:** Metallic
**Size:** Small

**Color:** Olive
**Description:** Metallic
**Size:** Small

**Color:** Chamois, sulphur yellow
**Description:** Pearl
**Size:** Small

**Color:** Yellow
**Description:** Pearl
**Size:** Small

**Color:** Orange
**Description:** Pearl
**Size:** Small

**Color:** Slate dun
**Description:** Pearl
**Size:** Small

**Color:** Crystal
**Description:** Translucent
**Size:** Small

**Color:** Orange
**Description:** Translucent
**Size:** Small

**Color:** Roe red, scarlet
**Description:** Translucent
**Sizes:** Small, x-small

**Color:** Green
**Description:** Translucent
**Size:** Small

**Color:** Dark green
**Description:** Translucent
**Size:** Small

**Color:** Root beer, brown
**Description:** Translucent
**Size:** Small

**Color:** Blue dun
**Description:** Translucent
**Size:** Small

**Color:** Peacock, emerald
**Description:** Translucent
**Sizes:** Small, x-small

**Color:** Burgundy, plum crazy
**Description:** Translucent
**Size:** Small

**Color:** Pink/pearl
**Description:** Silver-lined
**Size:** Small

**Color:** Ice blue
**Description:** Iridescent
**Size:** X-small

**Color:** Shrimp pink
**Description:** Iridescent
**Size:** X-small

**Color:** Copper
**Description:** Metallic
**Size:** X-small

**Color:** Pearl
**Description:** Pearl
**Size:** X-small

**Color:** Light apricot, chamois
**Description:** Pearl
**Size:** X-small

**Color:** Root beer
**Description:** Pearl
**Size:** X-small

## Bead Size

Glass beads are generally sized as "seed" for small and "pebble" for large beads. Sizes are identified by the " /0" system, which describes the number of beads per inch when the beads are laid flat on end, not strung. For example size 11/0 refers to 11 seed beads per inch. The following is a cross reference of the " /0" system to the current size system used in this book:

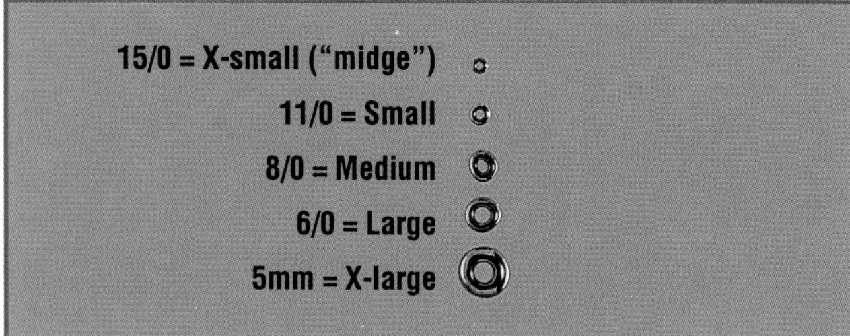

15/0 = X-small ("midge")
11/0 = Small
8/0 = Medium
6/0 = Large
5mm = X-large

There are five sizes of beads: extra small (or "midge"), small, medium, large, and x-large, that fit on hooks ranging from a size 24 to size 5/0. A hook's wire thickness is a significant factor when threading on a bead. For example, you might find that an extra small bead will slide onto a size 14 hook, 1X fine, but will not fit on a size 14 hook, 1X heavy (see "Hook Size Chart for Glass Beads").

**Hook Size Chart for Glass Beads**

| BEAD / HOOK | X-small (Midge) | Small | Medium | Large | X-Large |
|---|---|---|---|---|---|
| 1X Fine | 14-24 | 6-18 | 3/0-10 | 5/0-10 | 5/0-6 |
| STD | 16-24 | 10-20 | 2-12 | 2/0-10 | 3/0-6 |
| 1X Heavy | 18-24 | 14-20 | 8-14 | 1-10 | 1/0-6 |

**Note:** This hook/bead chart is used by permission of Temple Fork Outfitters, Inc. Hook styles and wire vary. Use chart as a general guide only.

## Bead Colors and Finishes

By no means are the beads shown here the full extent of bead selection. The beauty in glass beads lies in their color and finish. The preceding glass bead color plates represent color identification, description of finish, and the available size(s).

The bead's finish is an important element in the final appearance of your fly. Silver-lined (sl) beads show sparkle and glisten; metallic (m) and pearl (p) beads give luster and shine; iridescent (ir) and translucent (tr) beads glow and refract light, and inside color (ic) beads appear three-dimensional. In the materials list for each fly in this book, the abbreviation of the finish follows the color of the bead(s) is included.

## Tools and Accessories

When tying with medium or large beads, it is fairly easy to thread them onto a hook by hand. However, threading small or extra-small beads onto a hook is best accomplished by using a tool. I prefer to use the Bead Picker from Temple Fork Outfitters, Inc. The Bead Picker is a plastic ring with an adhesive patch that you dab into the beads. Then you simply slide the hook through the beads on the adhesive patch. The adhesive patch is replaceable. Mini hemostats and needlenose pliers also work, but they can be awkward to use. Another disadvantage of these tools is that you can only work with one bead at a time.

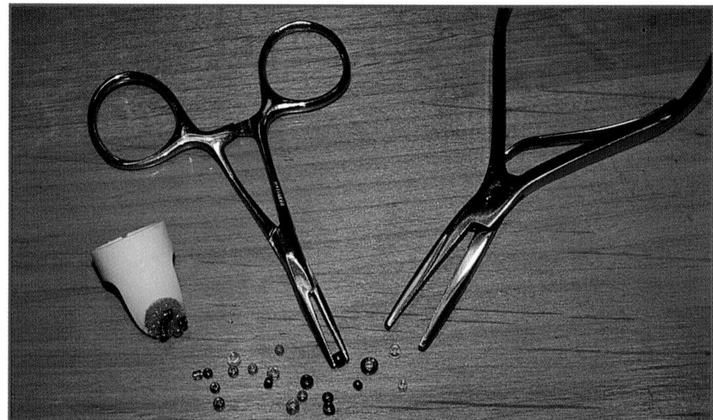

From left to right, the Bead Picker is the most convenient way to thread small beads onto a hook, followed by short hemostats or needlenose pliers.

## Bead Storage

If you store your beads in something other than their original packaging, pick your bead container carefully. Containers including the circular caddy pack or flip-top compartment boxes with separate compartment lids are the most efficient. There is no migration of beads to worry about, plus if you work with only one compartment open and the container is knocked over, at worst you will only spill the beads from that one compartment.

Hook boxes (such as the Pro-20 Hook Box) are useful as well, but make sure that the lid fits tightly to avoid bead migration from compartment to compartment, and that each compartment has a curved bottom for easy retrieval.

A small measuring scoop is a handy tool for moving or transferring a large number of beads at once.

Various types of containers for properly storing beads. Note small measuring spoon for dipping beads out of their compartment.

# Chapter 2

# Single Bead Flies

Glass beads earn their place among the gold, copper, bronze, or zinc beads that have made bead-head and cyclops nymphs effective and popular. Many fly tiers first used glass beads as an alternative to the metal beads used in bead-head patterns. The midge or X-small size bead is excellent for micro bead-head flies ranging from hook sizes 18 through 24. There is also the benefit of color and finish with glass beads. Weight is also a consideration because glass is not as dense as metal, which broadens the spectrum in the speed of sinking flies.

If you are familiar with tying metal bead-head flies, then you will find tying a glass bead-head fly to be just as easy. For this reason, you will not find one in the following pages of the tying techniques. Instead, you will learn five ways to improve and/or enhance a pattern with a single bead, whether you're tying a nymph or dry fly.

In the many years I have tied flies I've never figured out why so many patterns call for small materials for various parts, like tinsel for a tag, a few bright hackle fibers for a beard, a lump of chenille for the butt, or jungle cock feathers for the cheeks. I just assumed that these were more for cosmetic reasons than anything else until I attended a presentation given by John "Smurf" Smeraglio on fly fishing for steelhead on Oregon's Deschutes River. When John discussed the details on steelhead flies, he briefly mentioned the "target" concept, by which he uses a small piece of material, or an arrangement of materials, to stand out in the fly giving the fish a target to key in on for the attack. Having heard this, everything fell into place and finally the light clicked on. And all this time I thought the Green Butt Skunk was just another pretty fly!

The bottom line is that steelhead flies are not the only ones to incorporate the "target" concept, if you stop and think about it, the same thing is true when fishing bead-head nymphs for trout or adding great big eyes on baitfish patterns. In conclusion, a single glass bead may be applied as an excellent target anywhere on a fly whether it is used to imitate a gas bubble, egg sac, to highlight the thorax or the butt on a steelhead skunk!

## The Gas Bubble Bead Scuba Diving Olive

The Gas Bubble Bead Scuba Diving Olive was originated by John Ciulla, a trout fly fishing enthusiast and free-lance writer from Park Ridge, New Jersey. John's innovative use of glass beads provided the idea for using small, clear, silver-lined beads to imitate gas bubbles on subsurface stages of aquatic insects (as a result he trademarked his own product, Gas Bubble Beads).

It is interesting to note that John does not thread his beads onto the hook's shank, but rather threads the beads onto monofilament and manipulates it to where the beads should lie on the pattern. John introduced this technique in a 1993 article in *American Angler* magazine, "The Gas-Bubble Pupa", in which he tied several caddis pupae with beads as gas bubbles. He later developed the Gas Bubble Bead Scuba Diving Olive by imitating an adult blue-wing olive mayfly as it traps a pocket of air underneath its folded wings and enters the water to oviposit its eggs.

The Gas Bubble Scuba Diving Olive has been a successful pattern for John when catching brown and rainbow trout from the Beaverkill River and the east and west branches of the Delaware River. He prefers to fish the pattern in either a dead-drift or wet-fly swing.

### Gas Bubble Bead Scuba Diving Olive

***Hook:*** Daiichi 1180, size 18
***Thread:*** Olive 8/0
***Tail:*** Wood duck flank fibers
***Body:*** Olive rabbit dubbing
***Gas Bubble:*** Gas Bubble Bead (silver-lined finish) threaded on 7X monofilament
***Wing:*** Light gray poly yarn
**Note:** Colors may vary according to species.

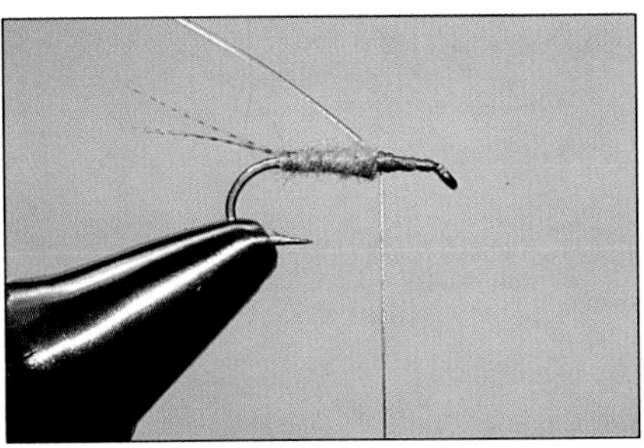

1. Tie in three split wood duck flank fibers for the tail and form a dubbed body just past mid-shank. Continue a thread base to mid-thorax and tie in a 3-inch length of monofilament (6X or 7X tippet material) securing the mono as you wrap back to the body.

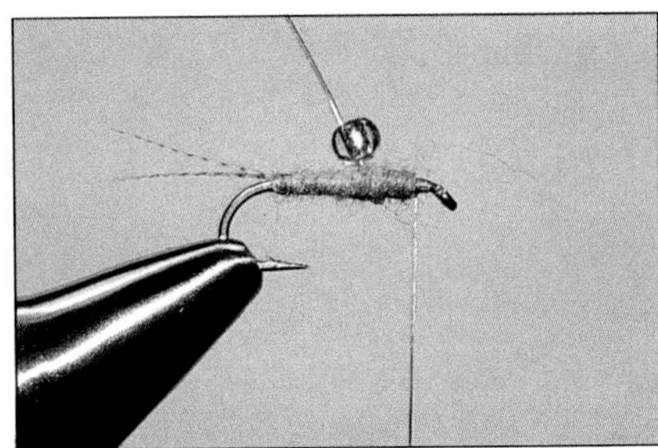

2. Thread a single Gas Bubble Bead onto the monofilament and add a couple more wraps of dubbing ahead of the bead.

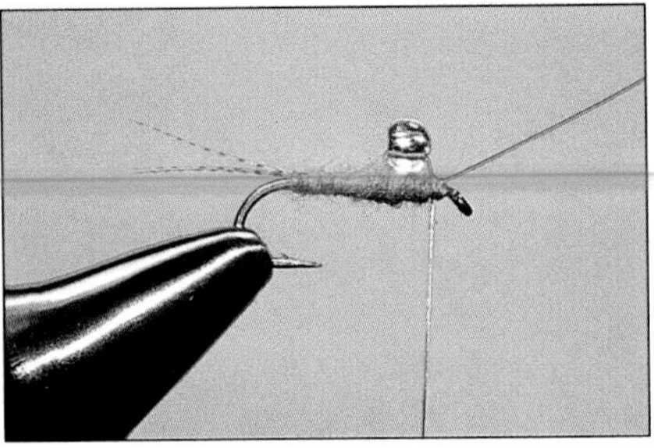

3. Pull the tag end of monofilament forward and secure with tight thread wraps behind the eye leaving room for the wing material. Trim off excess monofilament.

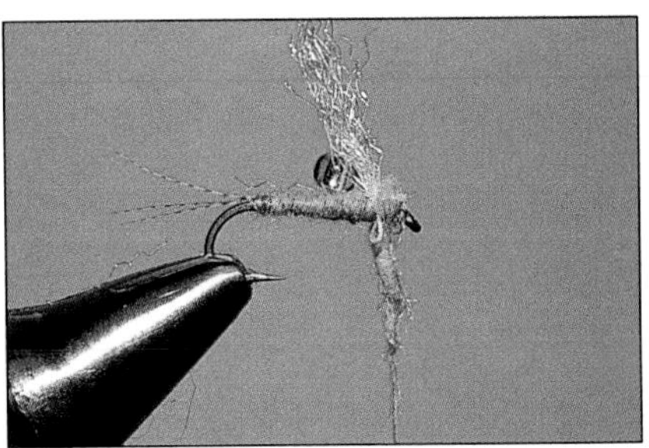

4. Position the bead at about a 45 degree angle and tie in wing material. Add a couple of wraps of dubbing and whip finish the thread. Trim the wing to 1/4 of an inch high.

## The Cripple Bead (*Baetis*)

The Cripple Bead was originated in 1994 by Bill Myers of Prineville, Oregon. Bill claims his sole purpose in fly fishing is to catch gargantuan trout on small flies, size 14 being the extent of a large size fly. You'll most likely find Bill trying to trick the more finicky trout laying in the flats of freestone streams.

The idea for the Cripple Bead pattern came to Bill while he was fishing one of his most cherished Oregon trout streams, the Metolius River. The fish were on a sipping frenzy to rising duns and, unfortunately, nothing from Bill's arsenal of tiny imitations was consistently enticing them (sound familiar?). It was time to get down and dirty and evaluate what was happening by collecting some live specimens for a closer view through a Mason jar. He noted two important elements of the small hatching mayflies: 1) the vertical profile of the hatch with wings and upper body extruding through the surface film, and 2) an air bubble that formed as the adult wrestled from its nymphal shuck.

After brainstorming at his tying bench, Bill created his impression of a crippled *Baetis* which included a glass bead to represent the air bubble by threading it onto the hook shank (*Note:* the glass bead was used after unsatisfactory results with plastic beads, Krystal Flash, and Cul-de-canard).

Bill suggests greasing only the hackles when using the Cripple Bead for an optimal presentation in the surface film; he uses it to stalk the "sippers" in slack waters. He has also created a *Callibaetis* cripple pattern in the same fashion which he uses for trout lakes and employs the "heave it and leave it" technique.

## Cripple Bead (*Baetis*)

***Hook***: Tiemco 900BL, Daiichi 1190, sizes 14-16
***Thread:*** Rusty dun 8/0
***Air Bubble:*** Crystal (ir) bead, small
***Body:*** Pheasant tail fibers
***Wing:*** Gray Z-lon
***Hackle:*** Dyed-green grizzly hackle

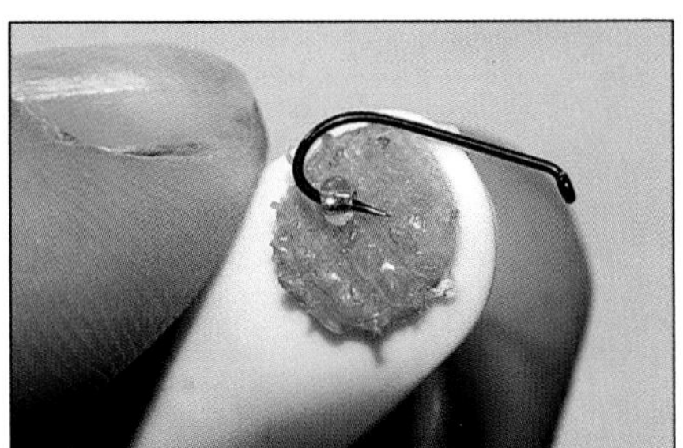

1. Slide one small bead onto a barbless hook before placing it into the vise.

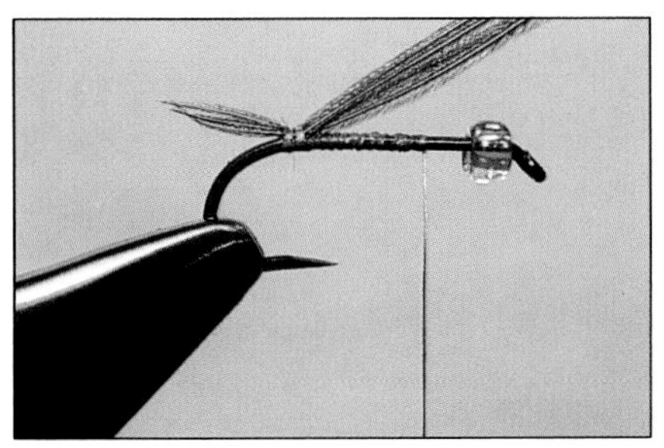

2. Slide the bead forward to the eye and tie in the thread behind the bead. Cover the shank with tight thread wraps to bend of hook. Tie in three pheasant tail fibers for the tail with butts long enough to form the body (color to match species); length of tail should be the width of hook's gape.

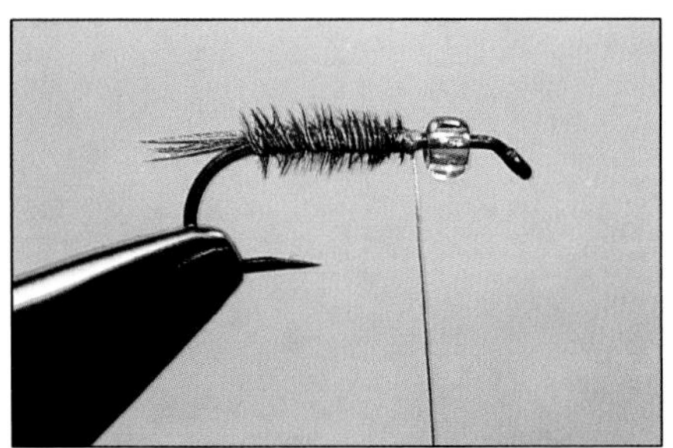

3. Wrap the thread 3/4 the way up the shank. Wrap all three pheasant tail fibers forward to the thread and secure tightly with the thread. Trim the excess butts.

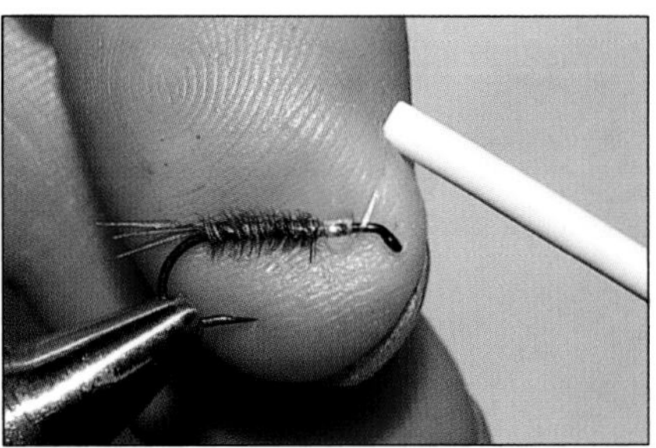

4. Push the bead up against the pheasant tail body. Hold the bead in place with your finger, bring the thread underneath the bead and wrap over the shank in front of the bead. Wrap the thread several times in front of the bead.

5. Advance the thread to about one eye-length back from the eye and tie in the wing material. Bring the thread back to the bead and tie in the hackle. Advance the thread to the wing.

6. Wrap the hackle to the wing and secure. Trim excess hackle. Whip finish in front of the wing and trim the wing material one-and-one-half times higher than the hackle fibers.

## D.B. Stimulator

The D.B. Stimulator is tied by Dennis "DB" Brown of Logan, Utah. This dry fly is an honest version of the Yellow Stimulator, a well-known pattern designed by Randall Kaufmann for imitating adult stoneflies. The surprising difference between the two patterns is the glass bead that Dennis uses on his. Personally, I find it quite remarkable that a glass bead can be used on a dry fly!

The idea of adding a scarlet bead to the Stimulator developed after Dennis noticed a bright red thorax on many of the mature yellow Sallys (a.k.a. little yellow stonefly) while guiding his clients for the cutthroat trout on the South Fork of the Snake River in Idaho. Dennis has creatively included glass beads in many types of fly patterns for quite some time, and is perhaps first to incorporate a glass bead in a dry fly. Why? According to Dennis, a single glass bead supports the target concept, that is, the bead is a highlight that draws the trout's attention and focal point of attack.

Dennis has also found that a single glass bead accurately represents the egg sac on egg-laying adults, which he uses on his Bead Butt Caddis. Inevitably, the first question Dennis is asked about his dry flies is, "Will they float?" The answer is always a resounding, "Yes!"

### D.B. Stimulator

***Hook***: Daiichi 1270, sizes 12-16
***Thread:*** Yellow 6/0
***Pre-Thorax:*** Scarlet (ir) Killer Caddis Bead, small
***Body:*** Bright yellow dubbing
***Body Hackle:*** Brown
***Wing:*** Light elk hair
***Hackle:*** Grizzly
***Thorax:*** Bright orange dubbing

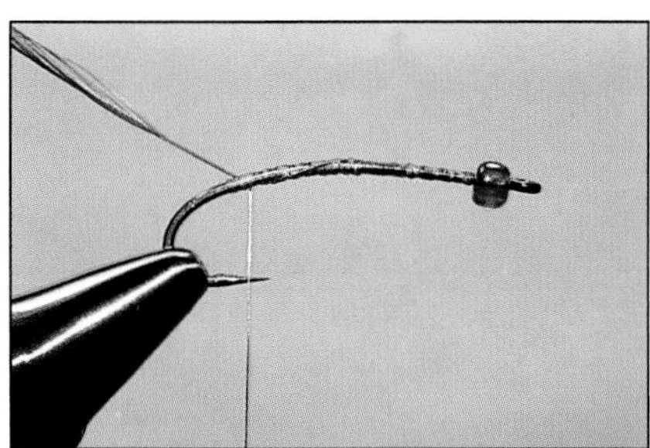

1. Use a barbless hook and slide a small bead onto the hook before placing it into the vise. Push the bead to the eye. Tie in thread behind the bead and wrap to the bend, ending in line with hook point. Tie in a hackle.

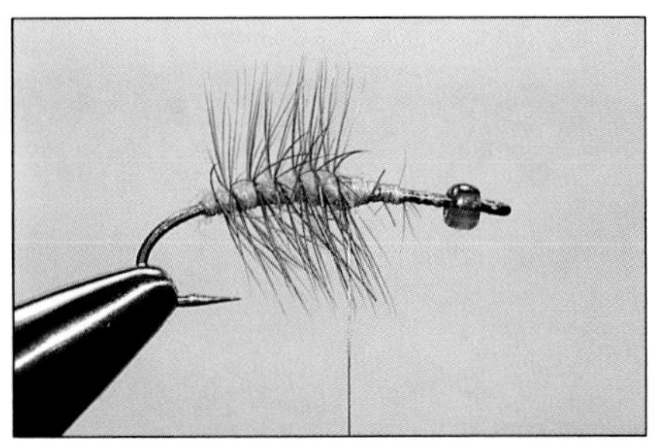

2. Form a dubbed body starting at tie in point of hackle to about middle of hook shank. Palmer hackle over dubbing and secure. Trim excess hackle.

3. Push the bead backward to dubbing and hackle. Bring the thread underneath the bead, over and around the shank several times to secure the bead. Tie in the elk hair for a wing (bead should be visible from the side view).

4. Tie in a grizzly hackle. Form a dubbing string for the thorax and wrap forward to eye. Palmer the hackle over dubbing and tie off. Trim excess hackle.

## Bead Banded Earthworm

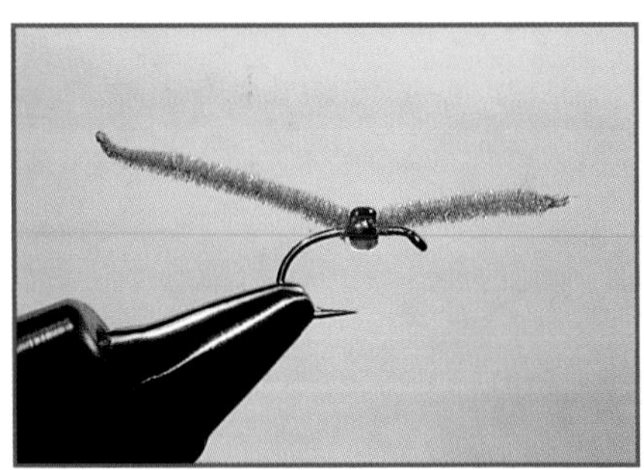

Undoubtedly this pattern is another spin-off of the famed San Juan Worm. Having seen so many creations of the San Juan Worm, I still can't figure out if the actual San Juan Worm is supposed to be an earthworm or bloodworm.

When I first tied this fly, I was going to take credit for it, but amazingly I stumbled across an article about worm patterns in *American Angler* magazine that had an exact picture of this fly. Unfortunately, there was no information regarding its name or who created it. For its lack of an existing name, I refer to it as the Bead Banded Earthworm.

I like to fish this pattern on a dropper system when nymphing for trout, and oftentimes it is the main taker. Once again the bead is used to represent a prominent part of the imitation, in this case the heavy band on an earthworm. Take note when threading the Micro Ultra Chenille through the bead, this could have many uses for other fly patterns.

### Bead Banded Earthworm

***Hook:*** Daiichi 1510, sizes 14-16
***Thread:*** Red 8/0
***Band:*** Root beer (sl) bead, small
***Body:*** Earthworm Micro Ultra Chenille (1mm)

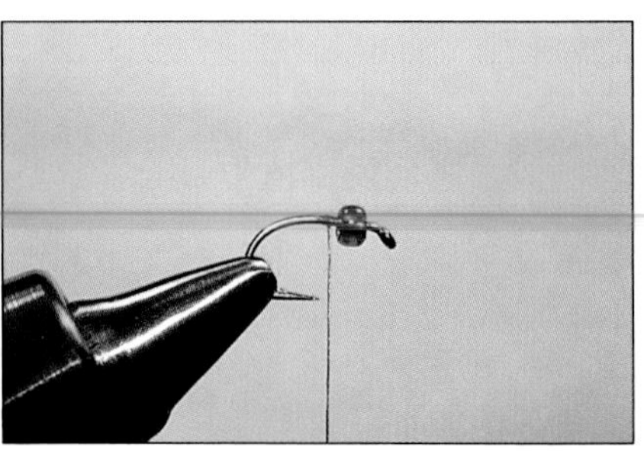

1. Slide a small bead onto the hook before placing it into the vise. Start the thread behind the bead and wrap the shank about the width of the bead, half hitch twice, and cut thread.

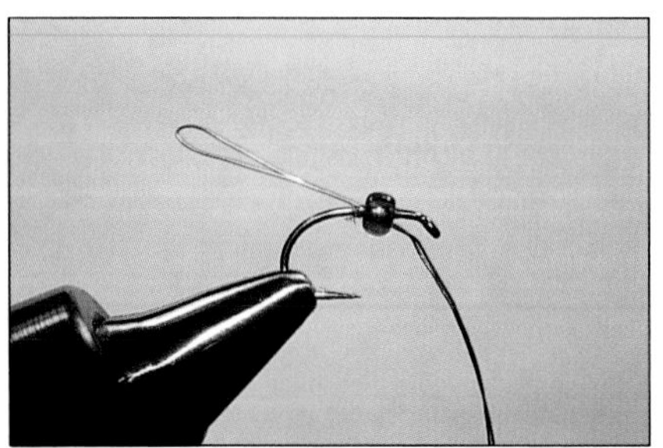

2. Use a fine piece of wire to form a loop and insert the tag ends through the bead, leaving an extensive loop on the other end to work with.

3. Use a length of Micro Ultra Chenille about one and a half to two inches long and either melt or strip the fibers off on one end of chenille. Insert the stripped portion into the wire loop and carefully pull the chenille through the bead.

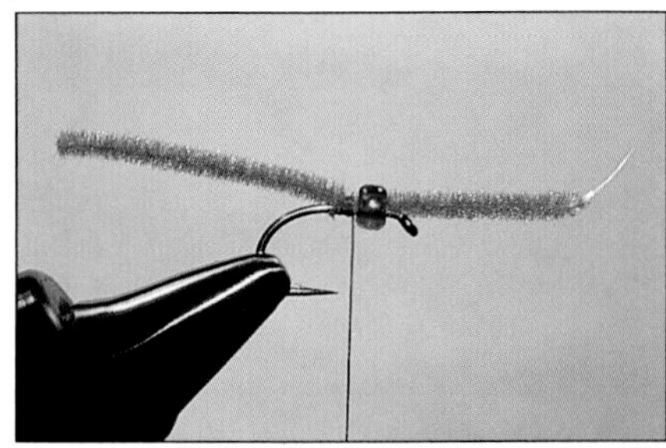

4. Attach the thread behind the bead and secure the ultra chenille atop the hook over the base of thread wraps. Slide the bead back covering the thread wraps and bring thread underneath bead to the front. Make a few wraps and complete with half hitches. Melt the ends of chenille to form worm-like appearance.

## Pettis' Unreal Egg

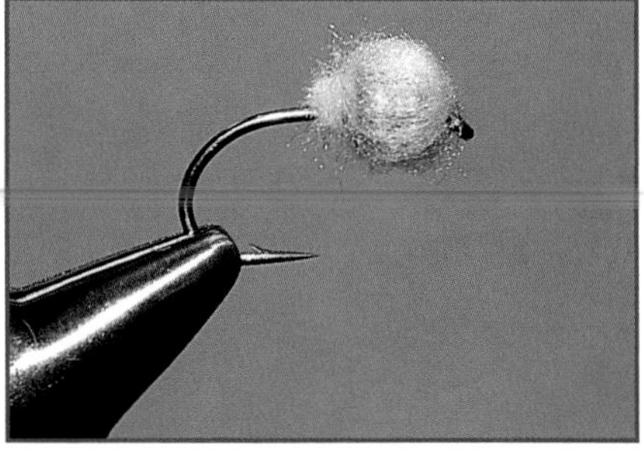

Fish egg imitations have been popular for many years and are extremely effective in stream fishing for resident and anadromous trout. One of the best-known egg patterns is the Glo Bug. However, in my opinion, none yield the lifelike impression as well as the Pettis' Unreal Egg. This egg pattern was originated in 1994 by Jim Pettis of Redding, California, who guides on the Sacramento River for the Redding Fly Shop.

The Unreal Egg is tied with traditional Glo Bug Yarn just like the original Glo Bug except the eye spot is formed by the bead within the yarn, which realistically imitates the nucleus material in a fertilized egg. Once the surrounding yarn is wet, the bead glows through it giving a three-dimensional appearance.

Jim's technique of enveloping the bead in yarn creates many possibilities for tying other types of flies, such as nymphs and attractor patterns. Jim also claims that the yarn has no sympathy for elusive light biters as the yarn becomes entangled in their needle teeth buying the otherwise deprived angler a second chance for a hookset before the fly is expelled. Although Jim has his favorite colored yarn and beads for the area he fishes, alter color choices depending on where you fish.

Pettis' Unreal Egg can be fished using standard nymphing techniques coupled with an indicator. Jim prefers to fish this fly on the end of a 12-foot leader and a Pettis' Unreal Roe (see Chapter 4) on the dropper without any additional weight and using an indicator for a drag-free drift. Using the latter technique, one should not overlook when fishing deep or fast-moving water.

## Pettis' Unreal Egg

***Hook:*** Tiemco 2457, Daiichi 1510, size 12
***Thread:*** Red 6/0
***Underbody:*** Dark orange (sl) or red (sl) bead, large
***Overbody:*** Peach king, champagne, apricot, or golden nugget Glo Bug Yarn

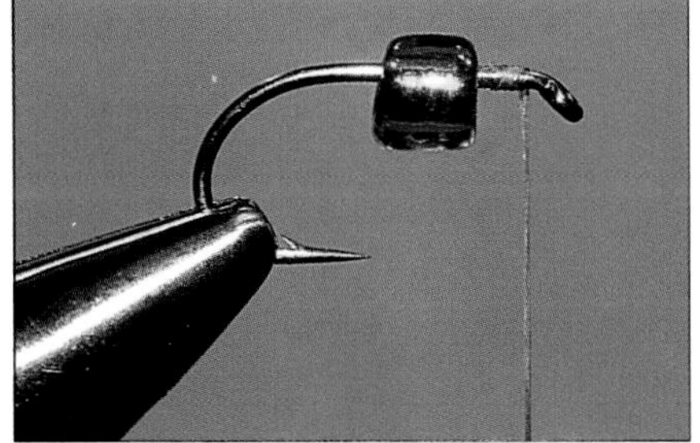

1. Slide a bead onto the hook shank and place the hook into the vise. Start the thread about two or three eye-lengths back from the eye and wrap forward to create a thread base.

2. Using about a half strand of yarn 3/4 of an inch long, insert center of yarn over the hook eye slightly extending past the thread base. Secure the yarn with tight thread wraps leaving a small tuft of yarn facing into the bead.

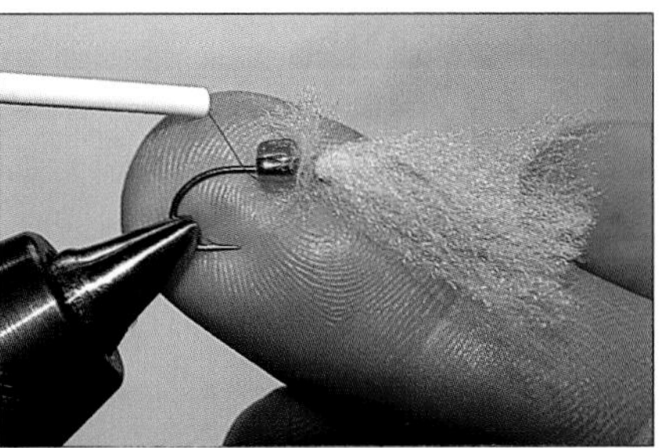

3. Slide the bead forward into the tuft of yarn and secure the bead by advancing the thread underneath the bead over and around the shank several times.

4. Using your fingers or a small brush, uniformly tease the yarn fibers away from the shank to create an even distribution around the bead when you pull the yarn back to drape around the bead. Loosely wrap thread around yarn fibers and the shank. Check for proper egg size before drawing thread tight. Secure thread with whip finish and trim excess yarn short to thread.

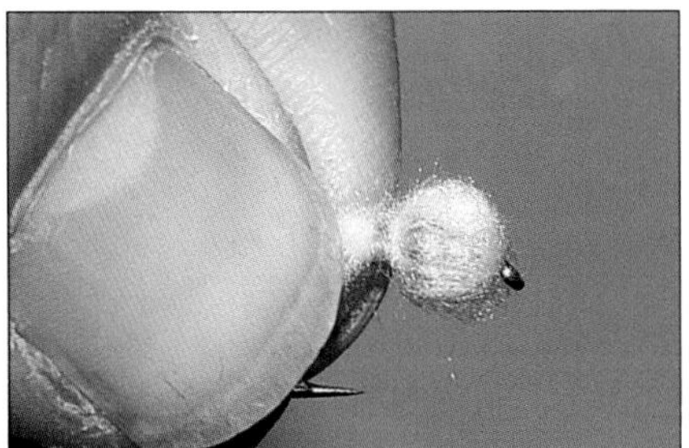

5. Using thumb and forefinger adjust whip finish forward into the bead. This will help hide the tie-off and true up the roundness of the egg.

*Chapter 3*

# Bead Body Flies

"Bead body" refers to flies that have more than one bead in sequence threaded onto the hook shank and where all other materials are tied in aft and/or forward of the beads. Substituting glass beads for conventional tying materials (dubbing, yarn, chenille, V-rib etc.) was my first use of large and small beads for the bodies on standard nymphs, attractors, and steelhead patterns. Bead bodies are not any more time consuming or difficult to work with than wrapping a body with traditional materials.

The pleasure of tying with beads is that proper taper, symmetry, and segmentation (ribbing) is already formed by the shape of the beads themselves. Bead combinations with alternating colors (such as black and silver beads) or sizes add even more diversity. Once the beads are in place, finishing the rest of the fly is no different.

The following bead-bodied flies will illustrate bead arrangement and the various options to help firmly secure the beads in place. Techniques vary according to the size of beads. The key is to firmly secure the beads on the hook shank, otherwise the beads may break.

## Killer Caddis

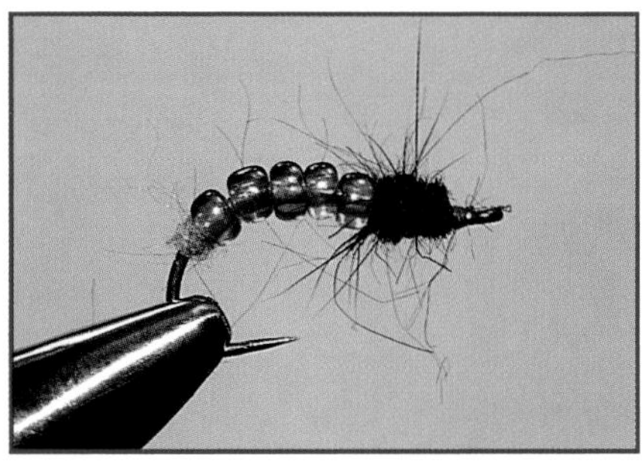

The Killer Caddis, which imitates a caddis larva, can practically be tied blindfolded, and its name is no exaggeration when it comes to proving its effectiveness on any given trout stream. The fly was originated by Dennis Brown in 1992 and is the start of Dennis' legacy of research and development using glass beads on a fly. The Killer Caddis is more than just a caddis larva, but rather, an all-purpose, "worm-like" larva pattern ranging in size from 12 to 18. I recommend using caddis green and/or peacock (emerald) beads.

Dennis has developed a special glass-bead hook through Daiichi (see hook chart on page 9) that features a barbless offset point, an extension of the shank for more room to keep the beads forward, and a closer gap between the eye and point for better holding. When Dennis designed this easily tied fly, he had in mind those of us who wait until the last minute to fill our fly box before we leave for our favorite trout haven.

### Killer Caddis

***Hook*:** Daiichi 1250, sizes 12-18
***Thread:*** Chartreuse at butt, wine to finish, 6/0
***Body:*** Three to five Killer Caddis beads (ir), small or midge, depending on hook size, color to suit
***Butt:*** Antron dubbing, color of beads
***Head:*** Black natural fur dubbing

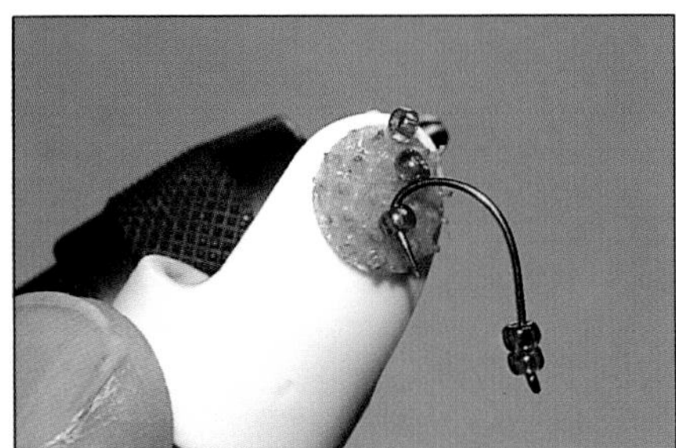

1. Thread 4 or 5 beads onto the hook shank (use 3 midge-size beads for hook sizes 16-18) and place the hook into the vise. Slide the beads up to the eye.

2. Start the chartreuse thread directly behind the beads and wrap the shank to slightly past the bend of the hook. Dub a small, tight ball of dubbing to form a button (the button should be smaller than the beads) and wrap the thread back to the beads. To size the head, use the distance between the dubbing button and the beads to gauge the amount of space left. Whip finish the thread behind the beads and trim (if the beads will not slide over the thread wraps, omit the second layer of thread and half hitch the thread after dubbing the button).

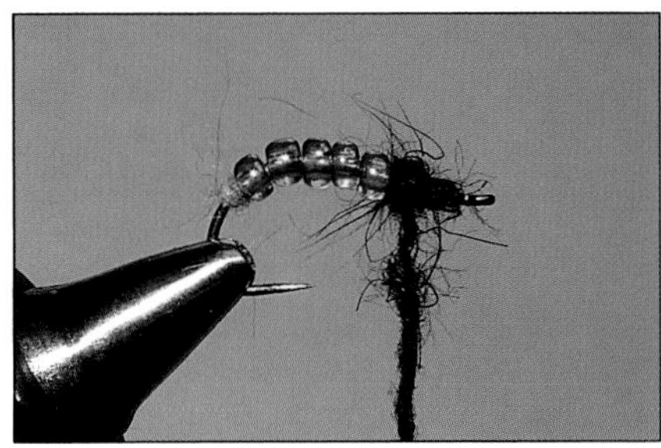

3. Push the beads back over the thread wraps and against the dubbing button. Tie in the wine-colored thread in front of the beads and dub a head. Allow the guard hairs to stick out to create a "buggy" look. The dubbed head should be larger than the diameter of the beads and taper smaller toward the eye.

## Metallic P.T. Nymph

The Metallic P.T. (Pheasant Tail) Nymph is my version of the Pheasant Tail Nymph with luster! But more importantly, it demonstrates the bead lock technique, used to secure beads onto the hook shank for durability. Although beads hold fairly well on their own, as illustrated by the Killer Caddis, the more secure the beads are the more durable they become.

The bead lock was developed by Bill Myers (originator of the Cripple Bead) and offers a quick and convenient way of using the tying thread to tighten and pull the beads together in a linear fashion, without the "out of place" look that comes from the beads not being perfectly cylindrical. When tying the fly, you never have to sever the thread or add a heavy thread base or dubbing at the butt of the beads to keep them from slipping off the hook.

At first, I was reluctant to try this technique because I did not like the idea of the thread being exposed on the surface of the beads and being vulnerable to chaffing. However, this became less of a concern when I began using Translucent Thread, a monofilament-like material from Spirit River, Inc. The Translucent Thread is invisible and more durable than typical fly tying threads. When adding materials like marabou or hackle in between the beads, the bead lock speeds up the tying process because you don't have to cut the thread in between each bead.

### Metallic Pheasant Tail Nymph

***Hook*:** Daiichi 1270, sizes 8-14
***Thread:*** Brown 6/0
***Body:*** Four or five brown or copper (m) beads, medium or small
***Tail:*** Pheasant tail fibers
***Wingcase:*** Pheasant tail fibers
***Thorax:*** Peacock herl
***Legs:*** Tips from wingcase splayed back

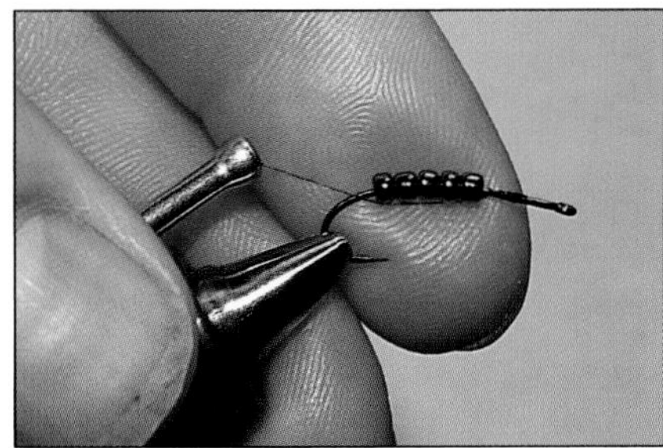

1. If necessary, debarb the hook for an easier fit for the beads. Slide five beads onto the hook. Place the hook into the vise and position the beads with your index finger to locate the body into position on the shank (leave plenty of space for thorax). Begin the bead lock by tying the thread at the front of the beads with several wraps and cross underneath all of the beads, bringing the thread to the back. Wrap the thread several times around the shank, use your right index finger to hold the beads in position and left hand to manipulate the bobbin; vice versa if left handed.

2. Tie in pheasant tail fibers for the tail and wrap several times around them covering the butts. Carefully push all the beads up against the thread wraps of the tail.

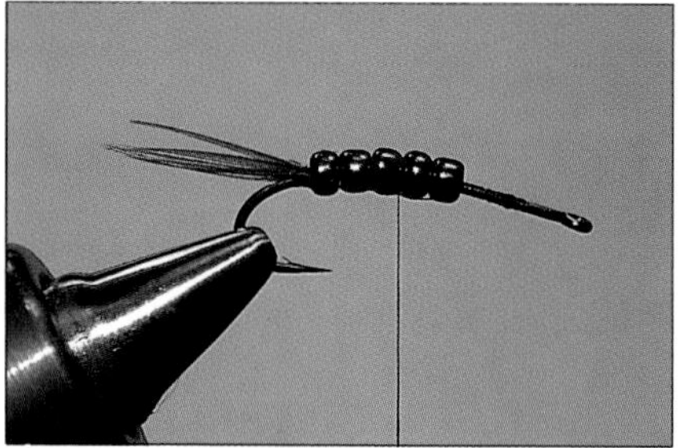

3. Advance the thread forward underneath each bead, one at a time, wrapping over and around the hook shank at least twice between each bead. To keep the thread from slipping over to the side use your finger to guide the thread.

4. Tie in pheasant tail fibers for the wingcase and peacock herl for the thorax. Wrap the peacock herl two eye lengths back from eye and secure with the thread. Trim excess butts. Pull the pheasant tail fibers over the herl and secure. Form the legs by splitting several tips apart from the wingcase fibers to each side and tying off with the thread. Whip finish the thread to complete the head.

## Joe's Drowning Ant

Most ant patterns are tied for a surface presentation, although they don't necessarily have to be at the surface for a trout to strike. Joe's Drowning Ant is a sinking ant pattern and once it hits the water and makes its descent in a tumbling stream, even the wildest brookie can't resist it.

Small mountain streams and meadows with nameless cascading beaver ponds are where I find solitude and a chance to have the trout all to myself. Perched on a fallen bleached-out fir tree that reaches into the muck of a tea-colored beaver pond, I quietly loft a short cast next to a fallen timber. The fly sinks a few inches, then from out of nowhere a scrappy eight-inch brook trout latches onto the sinking ant.

I developed this fly in 1995 as a stealthy terrestrial pattern for small turbulent creeks. Its use expanded to beaver ponds when I used the "what the heck, let's see if it works" approach. The fish snarfed it up! In addition to brook trout, rainbows have taken it too. Joe's Drowning Ant illustrates how you can combine different sized beads to create a tapered effect in conjunction with an off-colored bead to accentuate the fly and create a winning pattern.

### Joe's Drowning Ant

***Hook:*** Daiichi 1530, sizes 10-12
***Thread:*** Black 6/0
***Body:*** Black bead, medium; two black beads, small; and one black bead, medium
***Butt (optional):*** Scarlet (sl) bead, small
***Legs:*** Black neck hackle

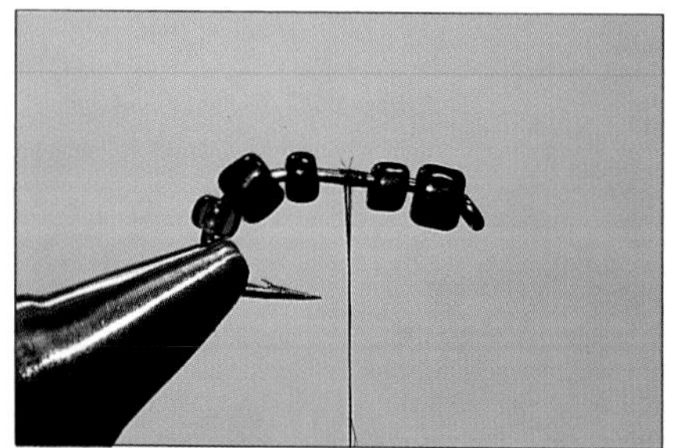

1. Slide a medium size bead, two small beads, another medium bead followed by a scarlet bead for the butt onto the hook and place it in the vise. Tie in thread in between the two small beads.

2. Advance the thread underneath the beads to the back of the last bead, over and around the shank several times. Bring the thread forward with two wraps between each bead until you are between the two small beads again. Use your finger to hold the beads in place as you wrap the thread.

3. Tie in a small neck hackle for the legs and advance the thread forward slightly. Wrap the hackle several times and secure with the thread. Trim excess hackle.

4. Advance thread forward to the eye of the hook wrapping a couple of turns between the small and medium beads. Whip finish thread to complete.

## Glass 'N Brass Goochie

I find great pleasure in streamer fishing big water by blind casting with a sinking shooting head system to work my fly right on the bottom. The jolting strike from a large trout or bass is exhilarating. One of my favorite patterns that frequently gets jolted from aggressive fish is the Glass 'N Brass Goochie. Oddly enough this streamer was developed for trout lakes and Columbia River smallmouth bass.

I prefer working with an olive color because many minnow-type fishes tend to have an olive coloration. I also like the gunmetal beads with black or purple marabou and Lite Brite; diamond beads with white marabou and Lite Brite are also a great combination. The brass bead is an optional part of the fly offering more sink, a jigging motion, and keeping the fly upright while it's being retrieved.

Anytime you use large and x-large beads you should prewrap the shank with a foundation using yarn, floss, etc. to help keep the beads secure and uniform on the hook. On his steelhead flies, Randy Babbitt uses wire chenille (a.k.a. pipe cleaner) as a foundation and extra weight under the x-large beads. When using iridescent or translucent beads, experiment with the color of your foundation to enhance or accentuate color. Also note that when dressing material between the beads you may not need as much material, if any at all, for the foundation.

## Glass 'N Brass Goochie

***Hook:*** Daiichi 1750, sizes 4-8
***Thread:*** Olive 6/0
***Bead Head:*** Gold or copper, medium (5/32) or large (3/16)
***Underbody:*** Yellow yarn
***Body:*** Four to six olive/pearl (sl) beads, large
***Tail:*** Olive marabou tips
***Wing:*** Chartreuse Lite Brite and olive marabou

1. Slide a brass bead onto the hook before placing it into the vise. With the bead at the eye, start thread behind it and cover the shank with tight thread wraps (at end point thread should align between hook's barb and point). Tie in a couple of yarn strands with the butts facing the rear (you may have to experiment with the yarn depending on how thick the strands are).

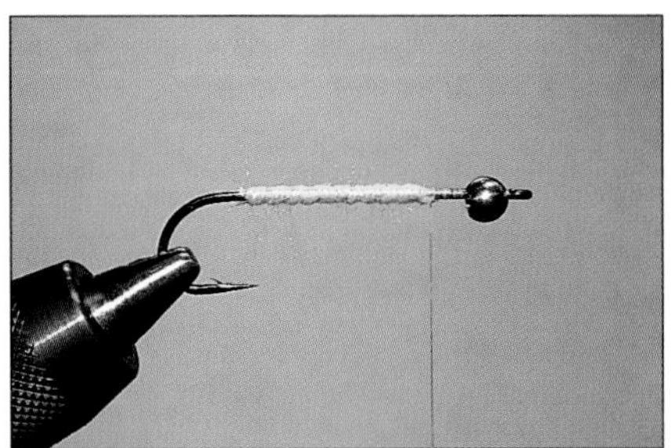

2. Advance the thread forward to the brass bead. Wrap the yarn forward, do not overwrap the yarn. Tie off the yarn about one bead length back from the brass bead (you need just enough space to tie in the wing material). Half hitch the thread several times and trim.

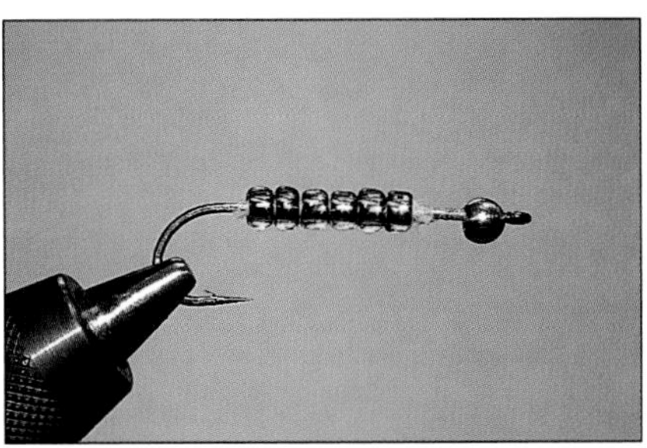

3. Slide the glass beads on over the yarn wraps covering most of the yarn. If the beads will not fit, this indicates that the yarn diameter is too large. Either use one less yarn strand or make certain that you have tight yarn wraps that do not overlap.

4. Tie in the thread behind the beads, secure the marabou plumes with wraps and finish with half hitches. Trim the thread. Don't trim the butts of the plumes too short to the thread, this will serve as an abutment so the beads will not slide off. Push the beads back to the tail.

5. Tie in the thread at the front of the beads and secure the Lite Brite material into position as a wing, the length should end just short of the tail.

6. Tie in the marabou plumes as the overwing, length should slightly exceed the Lite Brite but not the tail. Secure thread wraps and whip finish. Push the brass bead over the thread wraps and tie in thread at the front to form a head that will hold the brass bead in place. Whip finish the thread to complete.

## The Sultry Shiner

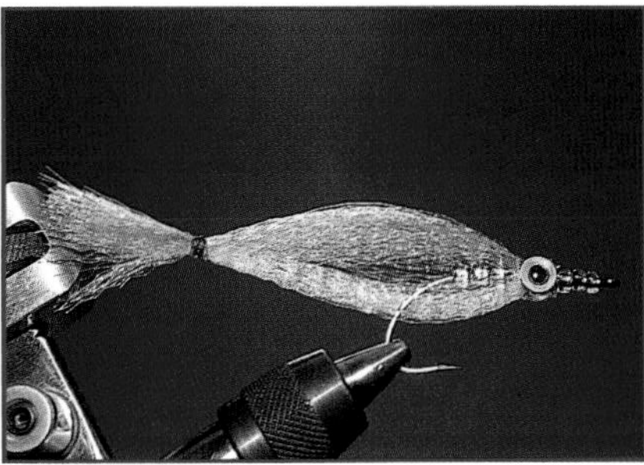

A smaller version of its cousin the Sultry Shad, the Sultry Shiner is a baitfish pattern I recently originated for bass that is suitable for any large piscivore (fish eater). The pattern is tied on a stinger hook which has a light wire and wide gap making it well-suited for beads. The Super Hair used on this pattern complements the beads by having a similar glow effect with light and forms a nice minnow-shaped fly. The hair fibers can be shaped to form the body by applying tension when tying the tail. The tighter you pull the Super Hair, the more streamlined the body will be; a slack pull creates a deeper-bodied fly. If you want to highlight certain parts of the fly with parr marks or spots use a black permanent marker. To firmly secure the rear beads I recommend using the bead lock technique.

The fly is well-balanced, rides upright, and does not drop or dip as a dead weight does. In fact, it sort of hovers on the pause of a retrieve. Attach the fly with a loop knot to allow it freedom of movement, and fish it with radical rod twitches to imitate an injured baitfish.

## Sultry Shiner

***Hook:*** Daiichi 2722, sizes 1/0-2
***Thread:*** Translucent Thread, fine
***Snout/Head:*** Two gold (sl) beads, medium; one gold (sl) bead, large
***Body:*** Three to five gold (sl) beads, large
***Belly:*** Green/chartreuse Super Hair
***Topping:*** Light green and olive (sparse) Super Hair
***Eyes:*** Yellow Lazer Eyes, small or medium, glue with Marine Goop
***Tail:*** Use olive 6/0 thread and tie off hair fibers about 1/2 to 3/4 inch back from end of hair tips and Super Glue
**Note:** This pattern is two to three inches in length

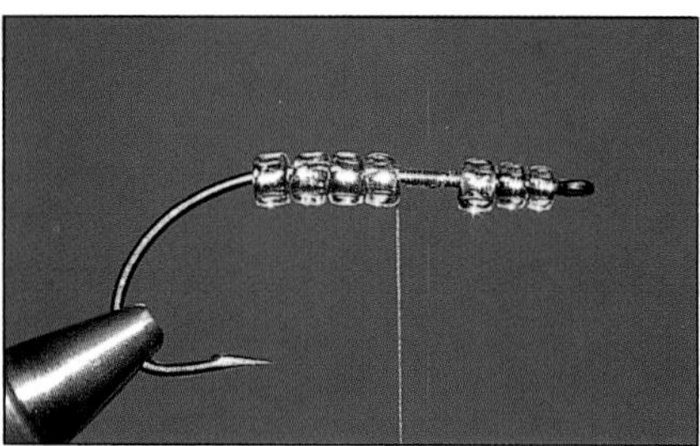

1. Pinch the barb flat and slide on 2 medium beads followed by 4 or 5 large beads. Advance the first 3 beads to the eye. Leave a space at least one bead width between the third and fourth beads. Tie in the thread behind the third bead and cover the shank with tight wraps.

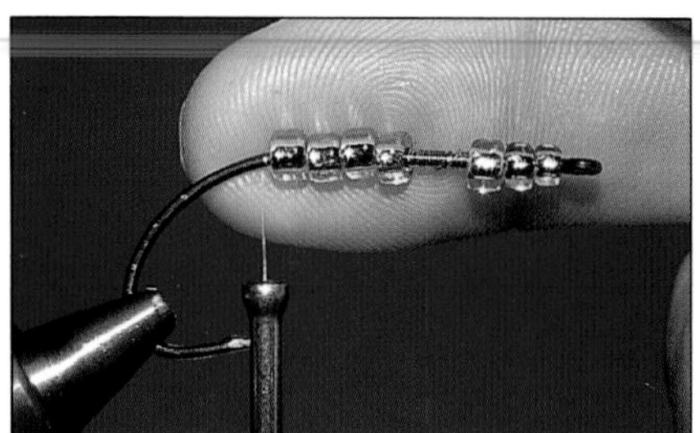

2. Apply the bead locking technique by crossing with the thread underneath the beads, over and around the shank several times at the back of the beads.

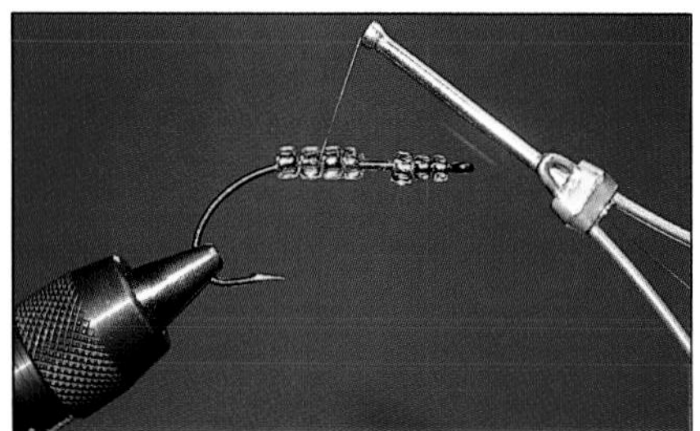

3. Advance the thread forward with two wraps between each bead until finishing at the tie-in point. Use your forefinger to keep the beads in place as you wrap the thread.

4. Rotate the fly upside down and tie in the Super Hair fibers (about 3 inches long) for the belly. Return the fly to right-side up and add the topping, light fibers first and dark fibers last. Whip finish the thread and trim.

5. Remove the fly from the vise. While clamping down with thumb and fingers to hold the fibers in place, grasp the fly at a side angle and pull the fibers back to form the shape of a minnow.

6. Tie in the thread by trapping the tag end with your thumb and wrap the thread four or five times with your free hand.

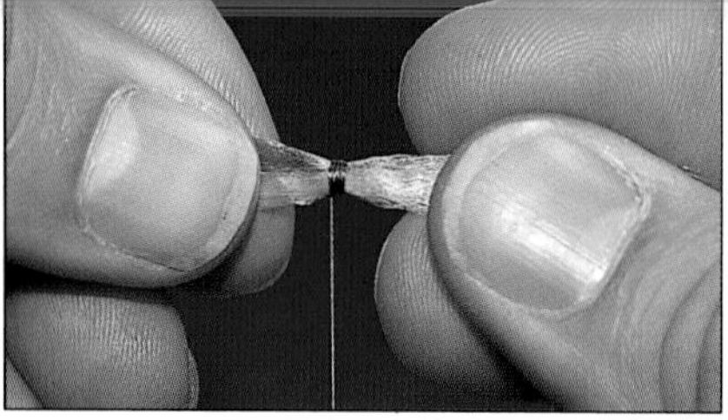

7. Grasp the fibers on each side of the thread allowing the bobbin to hang freely. Move your hands in small circular motions to twirl the thread around the fibers. This will form tight thread wraps. Whip finish the thread and trim.

8. Place the fly into the vise and glue on the eyes where the Super Hair fibers are tied in place concealing the thread wraps. Add a drop of Super Glue to thread wraps at the tail and trim ends of the fibers to shape the tail.

*Chapter 4*

# Dressed Bead-Body Flies

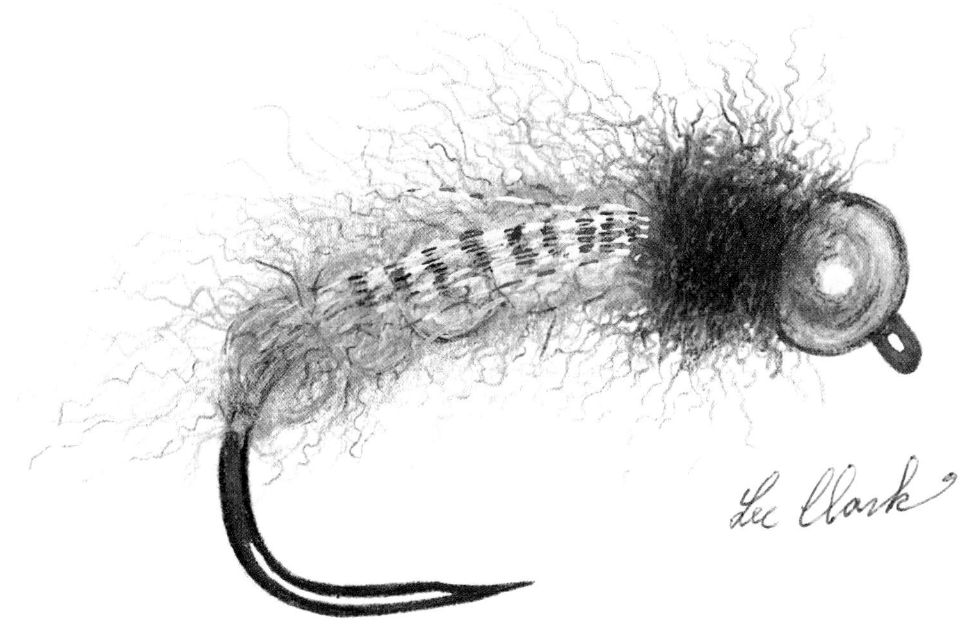


"Dressed bead body" refers to bead flies that are tied with materials between or surrounding the beads such as dubbing, Mohair, hackle, or yarn. Special effects are produced as light comes in contact with the bead causing a glowing or pulsating look through the materials, much like the transparency or sheen found on insects, fish, or crustaceans. Bead flies tied in this manner have a realistic look and are the most intriguing to create.

This is where beads receive the most attention for their use. With all the materials available today, I am sure that new patterns will be surfacing for quite some time. Dressed bead-bodied flies also add more protection for the beads.

## D.B Cranefly Larva

The D.B. Cranefly Larva was originated in 1996 by Dennis Brown. Dennis previously fished with traditional cranefly patterns made of ribbed dubbing, which is a standard imitation. However, with Dennis' growing experience using glass beads, the opportunity arose to create a realistic cranefly larva pattern. Using his bead weave technique he applied material within the beads for an added effect. The glass beads contribute symmetry and segmentation, and beads with the inside color (ic) finish appear three-dimensional. The addition of Mohair yarn between the beads provides silhouette and movement.

Daiichi's new larva hook tops off the pattern by giving it a nice shape. The bead weave is a very simple and quick way to wrap material (dubbing loops, Body Brite, hackle, or herl) between beads if you desire more than just the bead body style.

When fishing for trout during winter and early spring before the surface activity of hatches occurs, Dennis shifts to the big flies and uses his Cranefly Larva in a dead-drift through fast-flowing water.

### D.B. Cranefly Larva

***Hook***: Daiichi 1870, sizes 6-8
***Thread:*** Black 3/0 mono cord
***Body:*** Six blueberry (tr) or jalapeno (ic) beads, medium; one root beer (sl) bead, large
***Butt:*** Gray Mohair
***Bead Dressing:*** Gray or olive Mohair
***Thorax:*** Gray natural fur dubbing

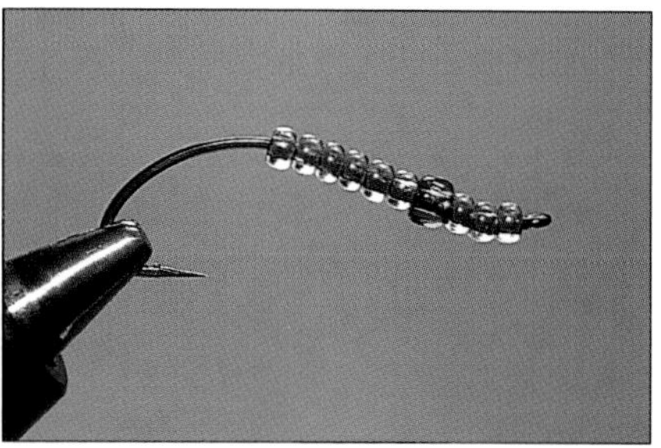

1. Flatten the hook's barb and place it in the vise at the middle of the hook's bend. Use needlenose pliers and open up the gap of the hook so that the point is directly in line with the eye. Remove the hook and slide on the beads up to the eye. Place the hook back into the vise at a slight downward angle.

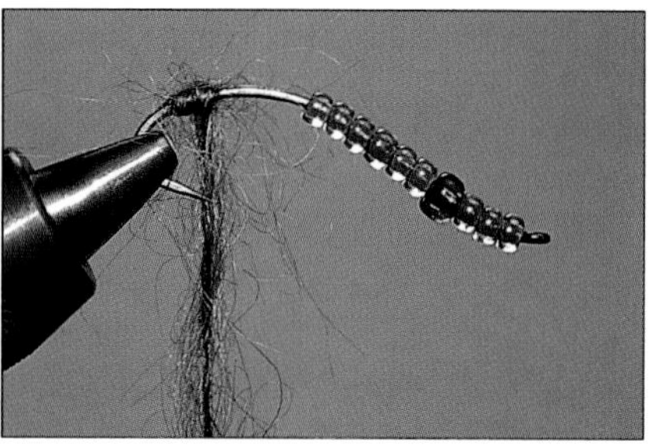

2. Tie in the thread at the hook bend and wrap a thread base. Tie in the Mohair yarn atop the thread base and tie off the thread with half hitches. Trim the thread.

3. Wrap the yarn over the tie-in point to form a butt. Slide a bead back against the base of yarn with your finger and hold it in position. Wrap under the bead and then over the hook shank. Slide the next bead back and repeat the process until you finish at the front of the beads.

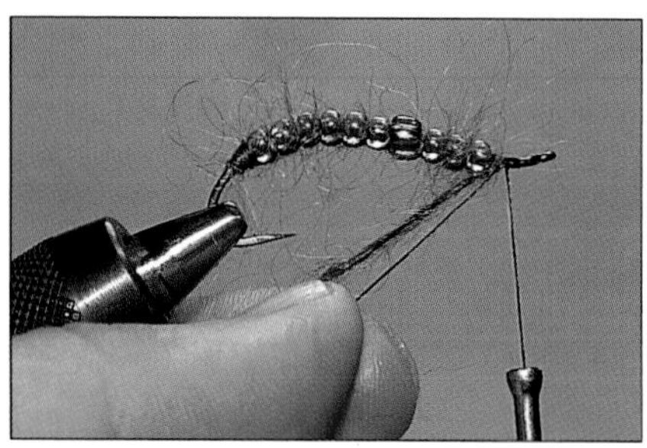

4. While holding the yarn tight with your left hand, grasp the thread and tie it just behind the hook eye. Secure the yarn with tight thread wraps and trim the yarn.

5. Notice that the bead weave of Mohair is directly underneath the beads.

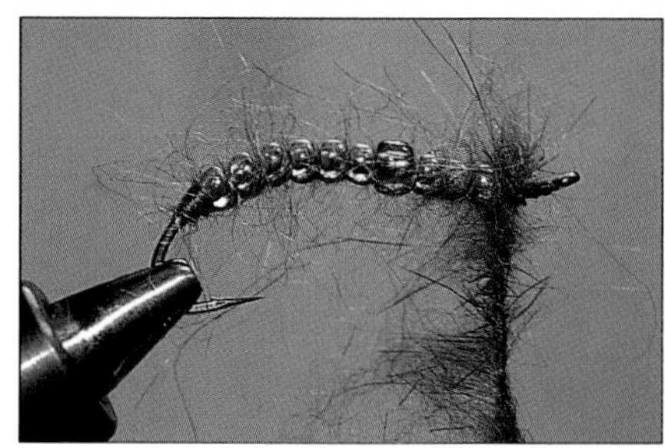

6. Form a dubbing loop and dub the fur so that it is very fuzzy and spiky. Pull the fibers back with your thumb and finger between each wrap as you form the thorax. Finish the head with thread wraps and whip finish.

## Pettis' Pulsating Caddis

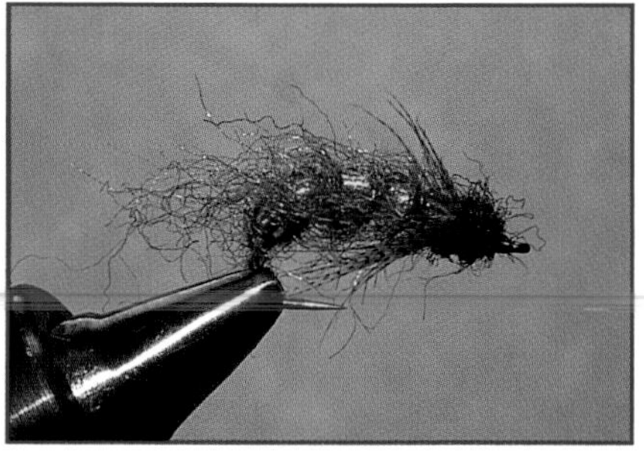

One great idea leads to another and so it was with the creation of the Pulsator Caddis. This pattern is Jim Pettis' first glass-bead fly. He originated the fly in 1993 after being inspired by John Ciulla's article, "Gas-Bubble Pupa". Jim opted for a slightly different approach for incorporating beads into his fly patterns. Both fly tiers have completely different motives for using beads, this helps show tiers the many different possibilities for using beads in flies.

Jim has set a trend by utilizing the light-absorbing characteristics in glass beads to give them a transparent look as he ties the materials in between and around the beads. Just add water and watch them come alive.

Jim ties the Pulsator Caddis as a pupa, pupa bead-head, and an emerger (all of which are pictured in this book).

The two prominent caddisflies, *Hydropsyche* (a net-spinning caddis) and *Brachycentrus* (a tube-cased caddis), that inhabit the Sacramento River near Redding, California, are a main staple in the diet of the very big rainbow trout that thrive there. I am certain that if you take Jim's lead, you can effectively match your local caddis, flies with the appropriate color scheme.

When the caddis are in season, try fishing the fly on the bottom (don't negate the use of split-shot) in early morning, the mid-water column in the afternoon, and in the evening convert over to Pettis' Pulsating Caddis Emerger for the surface action. Keep a firm grip on your rod!

## Pettis' Pulsating Caddis Pupa (*Hydropsyche*)

***Hook:*** Tiemco 2457, Daiichi 1250, sizes 12-16
***Thread:*** Olive 6/0, prewaxed
***Body:*** Four to six orange (sl) beads, small
***Bead Dressing:*** Lava brown Buggy Nymph Dubbing
***Legs:*** Wood duck flank fibers
***Thorax:*** Dark brown Buggy Nymph Dubbing

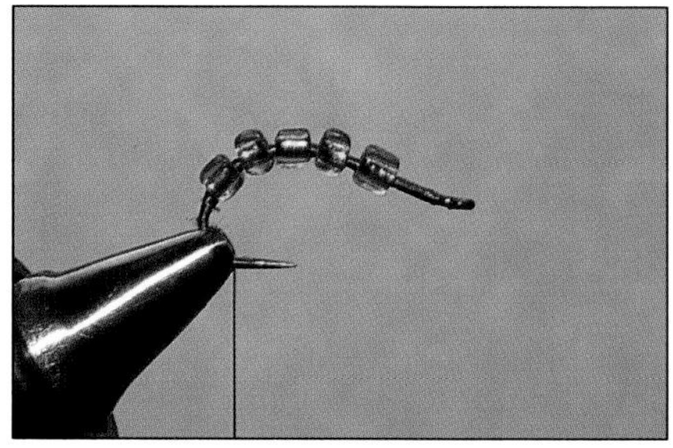

1. If desired, slide one small gold bead onto the hook followed by the glass beads and place the hook in the vise. Start the thread at the eye and wrap towards the beads leaving ample room for the thorax and head. Wrap the thread to the hook bend by securing the glass beads in succession with one or two wraps.

2. Form a dubbing string with a moderate amount of dubbing.

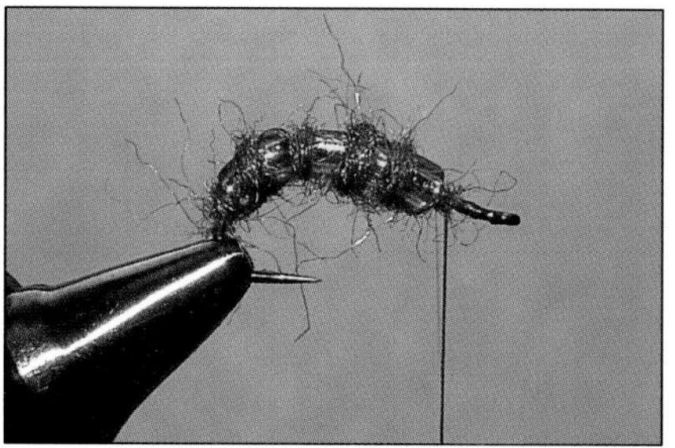

3. Dub forward with one or two wraps between each bead, gradually building the abdomen as you wrap to the front. Bring the thread ahead of the front bead and wrap several times to secure.

4. Brush the dubbing in a circular motion until beads are slightly exposed.

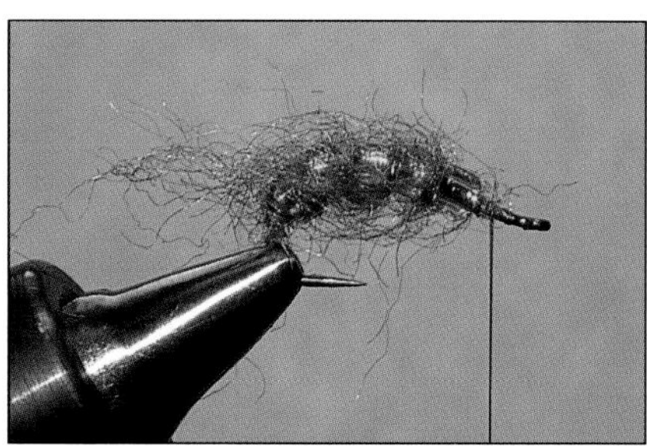

5. Gently brush dubbing to the rear to lay down fibers (author's Note: the fingers work well, too).

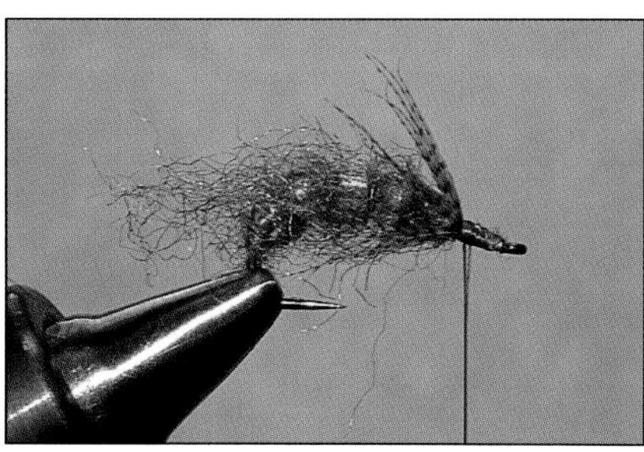

6. Tie in 8-12 wood duck fibers per side. Spread the fibers in a fan-like array and secure them with tight thread wraps.

7. Add dubbing material to the thread and wrap forward to form the thorax. Whip finish the thread to complete the head.

## Rainy's Bead Back Scud

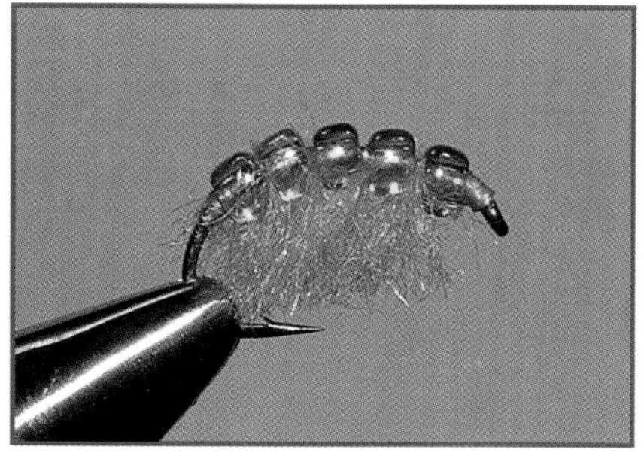

Scuds are also known as freshwater shrimp and are a part of the hard shell group of organisms called crustaceans. Scuds tend to be very prolific in many habitats, ranging from streams to lakes, that typically hold trout. Their abundance, combined with a high protein content, greatly contribute to a trout's rapid growth.

The Bead Back Scud was originated in 1994 by Rainy Riding of Logan, Utah. Rainy is a "vision" fly tier, that is to say, her personal patterns evolve while she sleeps. While it is still fresh in her mind, she wakes and heads for the tying table. Rainy claims that the Bead Back Scud came about during a 3 a.m. excursion. I'm guessing that her nightstand is adequately equipped and ready to go.

As you can see from the scud picture above, the beads resemble their thin transparent shell. The legs on the Bead Back Scud are an additional feature that contribute to the uniqueness of this pattern by using synthetic dubbing which does not open up large gaps between the beads. The coloration of scuds varies from region to region as the color is often a refection of the scud's diet. Their colors range from shades of olive to tan or gray.

## Rainy's Bead Back Scud (dark amber)

***Hook:*** Dai-Riki 135, Daiichi 1150 or 1250, sizes 12-16
***Thread:*** Color to match beads, 8/0
***Body:*** Five or six beads, small, color to suit
***Legs:*** Rainy's Sparkle Dub, color to match beads

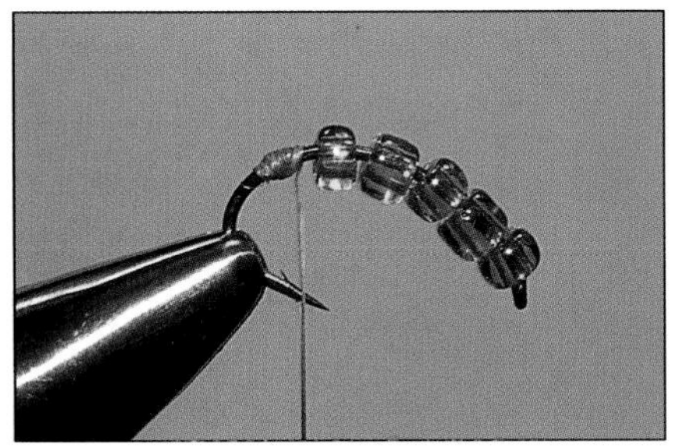

1. Thread 4 or 5 beads onto the hook and place it in the vise at a slight downward angle. Push the beads forward to the eye. Tie in the thread at the bend of the hook at least one bead width behind the beads and create a thread butt large enough to keep the beads from slipping off the hook, whip finish the thread and trim.

2. Push one bead back to the thread butt and tie in the thread. For the legs, collect a small amount of dubbing and form a noodle-shaped body by rolling the material between your thumb and index finger (dubbing should be an inch long and half the diameter of a bead).

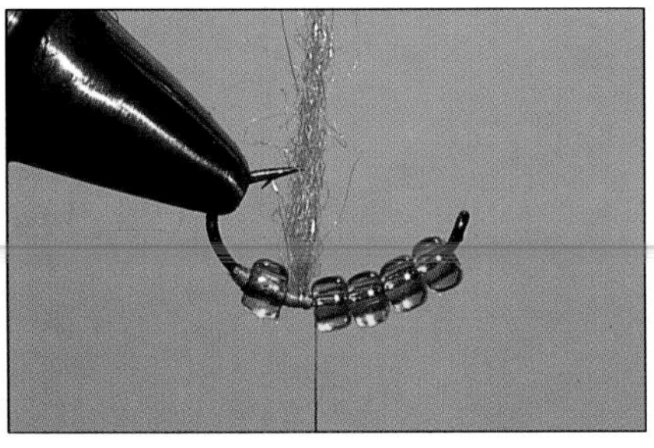

3. Rotate the hook so it is upside down. Tie in the dubbing strand by its center and secure with figure-eight wraps. Tie a couple of half hitches with the thread and trim. Do not overwrap the thread, this causes too much bulk which prevents the beads from closing tightly together.

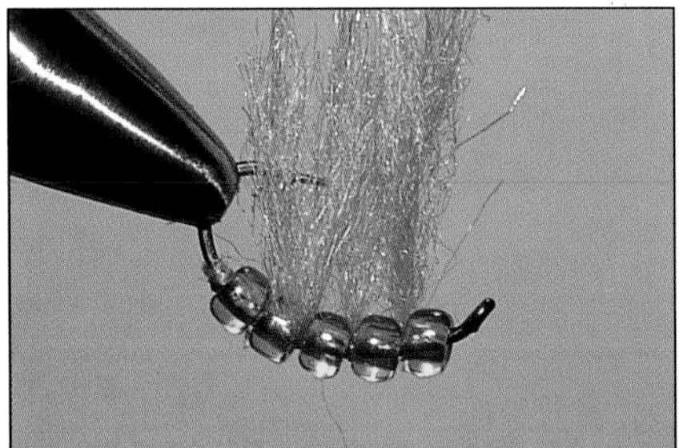

4. Push the next bead tightly against the dubbing and tie in the thread again. Form another dubbing strand and secure into place as described above. Repeat this step until you have completed the legs in between the beads. Tie in the thread between the front bead and the eye to finish the head with wraps and whip finish.

5. After the legs are completed, rotate the fly back into the upright position. Use a fine-bristled brush and comb the dubbing fibers down to form the legs. Trim the tips of the dubbing fibers to the width of hook's gape.

## Glass 'N Brass Surf Crab

The Glass 'N Brass Surf Crab is a spin-off of Jay Murakoshi's Bead-head Sand Crab which imitates the Pacific mole crab, a primary prey of Pacific Coast surf perch. To date, I have not had the opportunity to fish this fly in the surf, but I offer the idea of using beads as an excellent way to imitate the translucent underside of saltwater crustaceans.

The Glass 'N Brass Surf Crab also illustrates the hackle effect between the beads. For bead fly patterns that call for hackle between the beads, it is best to tie off and trim the hackle before advancing to the subsequent beads. This keeps the hackles durable and is stronger than wrapping it through the beads. If you want the hackles to sweep back like they do on a Woolly Bugger, tie in the hackle about half a bead width in front of the bead using only two or three wraps of hackle and push the following bead back slightly over the hackles (you should see the hackle tips begin to close towards the body). Use the same hackle repeatedly, starting with the tip to form a taper. To speed things up, you can advance the thread forward using the bead lock technique.

### Glass 'N Brass Surf Crab

***Hook:*** Daiichi 2546, sizes 2-6
***Thread:*** Olive 6/0
***Bead Head:*** Brass bead, medium (5/32) or large (3/16)
***Body:*** Four olive/pearl (sl) beads, large
***Tail/ShellBack:*** Dark olive Lite Brite
***Legs:*** Hot orange grizzly hackle wrapped between beads

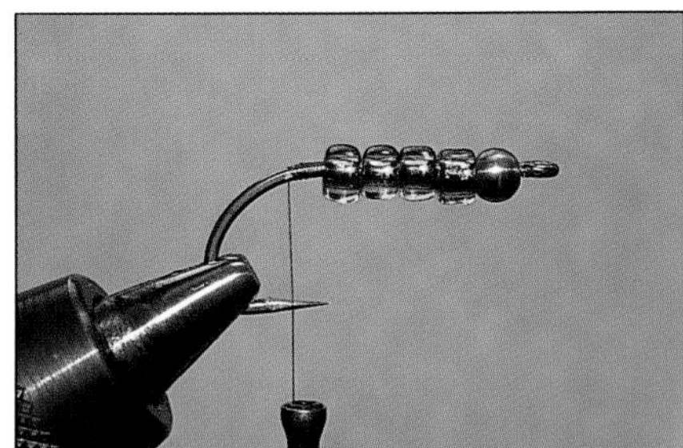

1. Flatten the barb and slide on a brass bead followed by 4 large glass beads. Place the hook in the vise. Tie in the thread at the back of the hook behind the glass beads and form a thread base to the start of the bend for the tail.

2. Tie in a small clump of Lite Brite for the tail (the length of the hook's gape) leaving enough material to pull over and extend past the eye. Push back and hold one bead with your finger and advance thread underneath the bead and around the hook shank; make several wraps with the thread.

3. Tie in the hackle (doesn't matter how you face it) and palmer about two or three times around the shank. Secure with thread and finish with half hitches. Trim excess and continue to use the same hackle. The hackle fibers should not exceed the gape of the hook. Advance the thread underneath to the next bead.

4. Repeat the procedure of the hackle twice more until you have reached the front glass bead. Wrap the thread forward and between the glass bead and brass bead.

5. Pull the Lite Brite fibers over the top of the beads and hackle and secure with the thread. Whip finish the thread and trim. The fibers out the front should be about the same length as the tail fibers.

## Pettis' Unreal Roe

Jim Pettis was on a roll when he tied the Unreal Egg. If there was to be a single-bead egg pattern there had to be a cluster of roe to go with it, hence, Pettis' Unreal Roe. The steelhead devour it and resident rainbow trout won't pass it up either. For extra weight on the fly, and not on the leader, Jim will use up to five glass beads for this pattern allowing for its quick descent. When tying in the beads, he recommends that the beads be kept on top of the shank as much as possible to avoid closing the hook gap.

Fishing egg patterns for scavenging trout during the fall chinook spawning season is too good to pass up. Jim sets up his leader by tying the Unreal Roe on the dropper and the Unreal Egg at the end of the tippet, and presents it with a nymphing drag-free drift using an indicator. When the fish see this coming they're thinking, "omelet!"

### Pettis' Unreal Roe

***Hook:*** Tiemco 2457, Daiichi 1530, size 10, barbless
***Thread:*** Cream Super Thread
***Underbody:*** Three to five orange (tr) beads, large
***Overbody:*** Early Girl (light roe), McRoe (dark roe), or pink McFlyFoam Bug Yarn

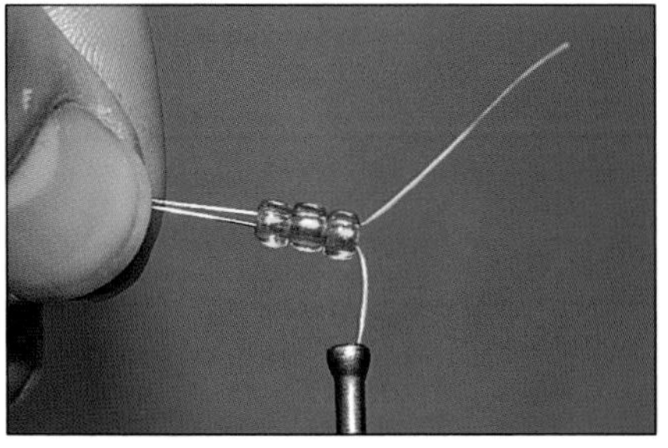

1. Fill a standard bobbin threader with glass beads. Thread three beads onto the thread.

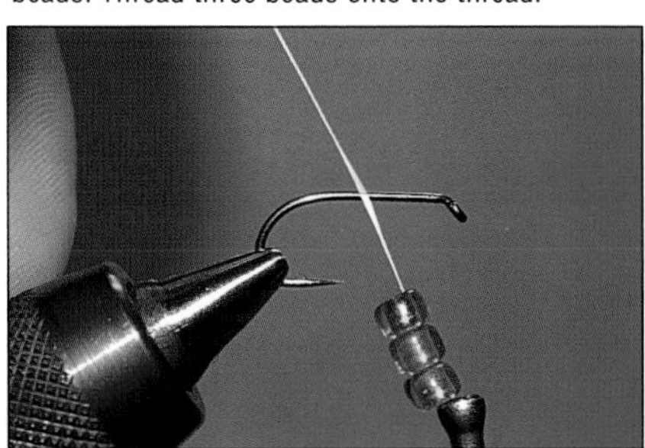

2. Start about the center of the hook and build a small thread base while holding the beads against the bobbin.

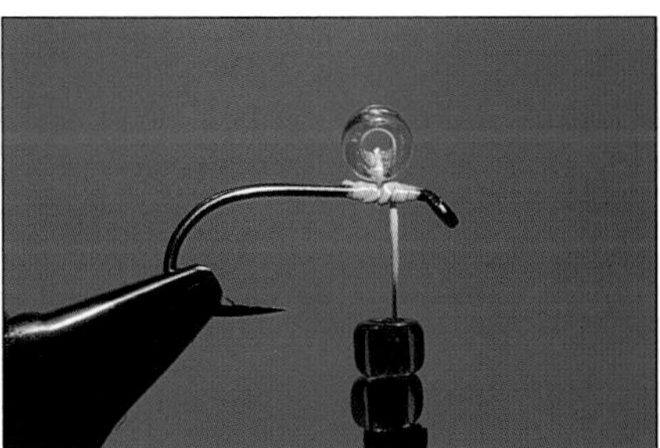

3. Let one bead drop to the hook shank at a time and secure it to the top side of the hook shank.

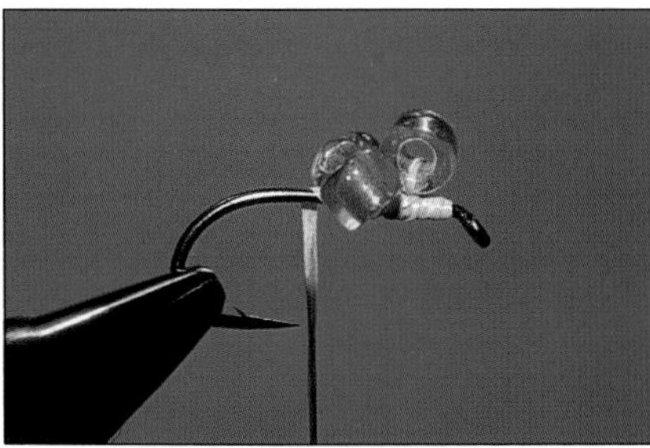

4. Repeat the procedure with the next two beads and tie them offset from the first one. Do not allow them to slip to the bottom of the shank. Wrap the thread several times around and under the beads and over the hook shank to firmly secure the beads. Advance the thread to the front of the beads.

5. Secure a portion of the McFlyFoam to the hook just in front of the beads, if you have tufts protruding out don't worry about trimming them off.

6. Advance the thread to the rear of the beads. Tease the foam so it is evenly distributed around the shank and draw the material over and between the beads leaving them fully exposed. Secure the material with snug thread wraps.

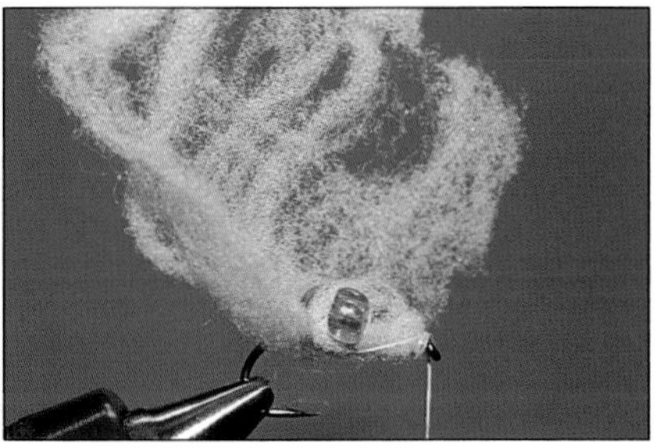

7. Advance the thread to the front of the beads. Tease the foam completely by creating a thin veil. Bring the veil forward so that it encapsulates the beads (the covering foam should be loose enough to give body and thin enough to allow translucence). Secure the foam with the thread and whip finish.

*Chapter 5*

# Extended Bead-Body Flies

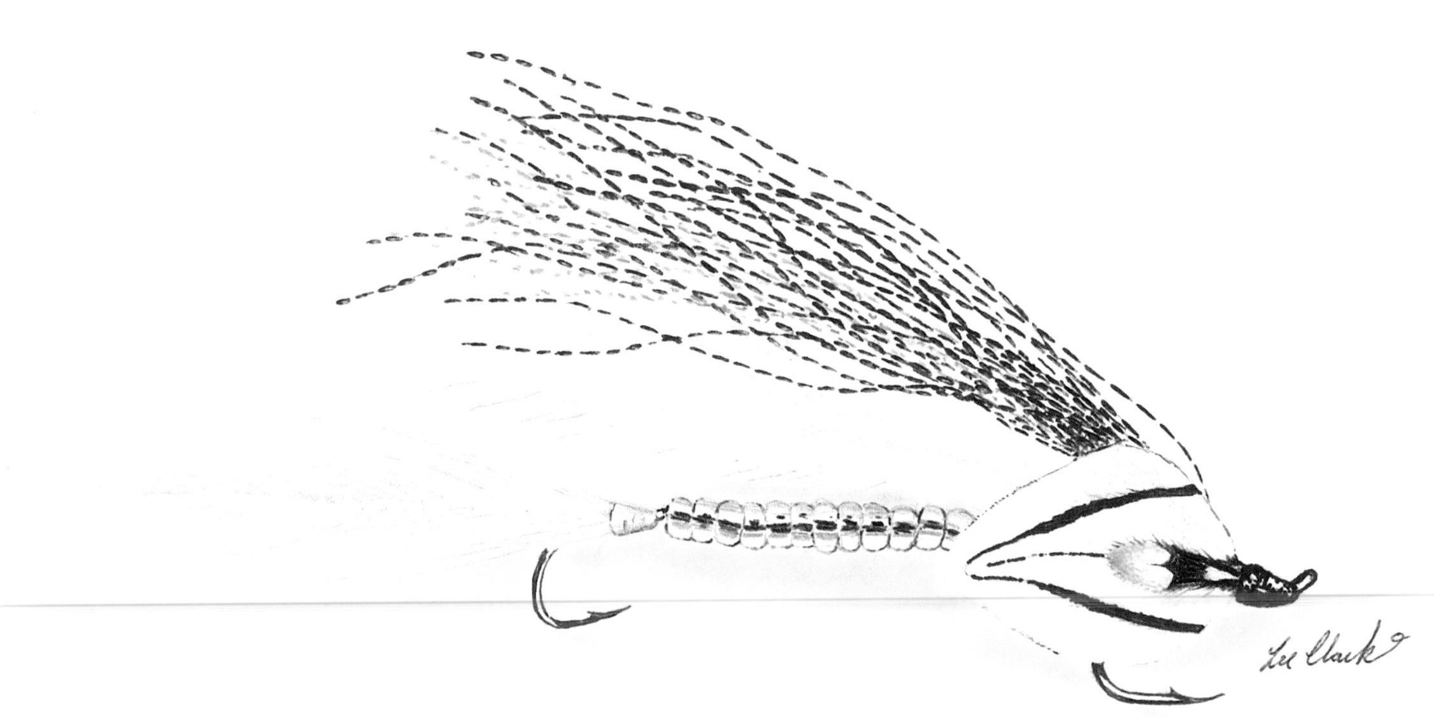

"Extended bead body" refers to threading the beads on something other than the hook itself. By doing so, you can attain more length without long shank hooks and also provide movement, such as an oscillating tail. Smaller beads will not thread onto large hooks, however you can overcome this by threading the beads on small diameter materials, such as wire, monofilament, ultra chenille, or rubber hackle, and then attaching this to the hook.

For attractor, streamer, and baitfish patterns, stainless steel, nylon-coated wire (American Fishing Wire) is excellent. The wire is very durable and the crimping sleeve provides a solid foundation for tying on a tail by either forming a slip loop and inserting the materials into it, or simply tying the tail fibers directly onto the crimping sleeve itself. Adding a trailer hook is a quick step, just loop the wire through the eye and thread on some beads.

# The Boogie Damsel

Wiggle or swivel flies tied with a pivoting point are a little more time-consuming on the vise, but the action afforded to the fly can be well worth the extra effort. If you are a person who likes to add life to your fly by puppeteering, you will find great benefits to this pattern. Not only will it provoke trout but also the inhabitants of warm-water ponds and lakes, such as panfish and bass.

For the swiveling body on this fly, use those old crummy hooks that are cheap or too dull to sharpen. If you specifically purchase hooks for the body of a wiggle fly, I recommend the Aberdeen-style hook that comes with a long, light wire shank and straight eye. Also notice the way the eyes are made using beads; fast and simple. Construct perfect eyes every time using extra small through large size beads in the many available colors, like scarlet, gunmetal, or emerald.

Fish the Boogie Damsel by letting it sink to the bottom and begin the retrieve one of several ways; rapid, one-inch strips (keep the rod tip down to the water's surface), short rod twitches either up and down (drawing in the slack when dropping the rod tip down), or from the side. If the fish are frequently cruising by, time the retrieve off the bottom so that the fly comes into the fish's view.

## Boogie Damsel

***Hook:*** Daiichi 1530, sizes 10-12 for thoracic
***Thread:*** Light olive 8/0
***Body:*** Seven or eight light green, olive/pearl (tr or sl) or gold (sl) beads, small, threaded on a size 12 Aberdeen hook, and 12-pound test mono to make the connection to thorax
***Tail:*** Light olive marabou tip fibers
***Wingcase:*** Light olive marabou
***Thorax:*** Olive shade to suit, hare dubbing
***Legs:*** Dyed yellow or olive guinea
***Eyes:*** Burgundy (tr) or peacock green (tr) beads, small, mounted on 20-pound test mono
***Head:*** Olive shade to suit, hare dubbing

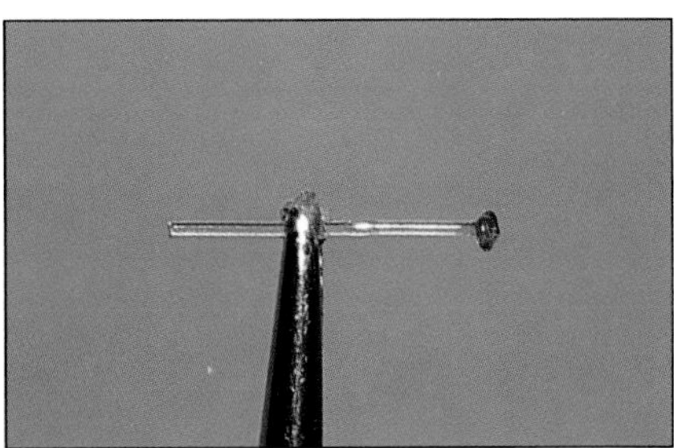

1. Prepare the damsel's eyes by cutting off a piece of monofilament (mono) about three-fourths of an inch long. Hold the mono with a pair hemostats and melt one end of the mono (a cigarette lighter works great). If you blow on the end immediately, while the mono is still hot, the tip will flatten to form a dish shape.

2. Slide two small glass beads onto the mono against the melted end and grasp the mono with the hemostats on the opposite side of the beads leaving enough of a tag to melt into a button. Close off the end by melting the mono.

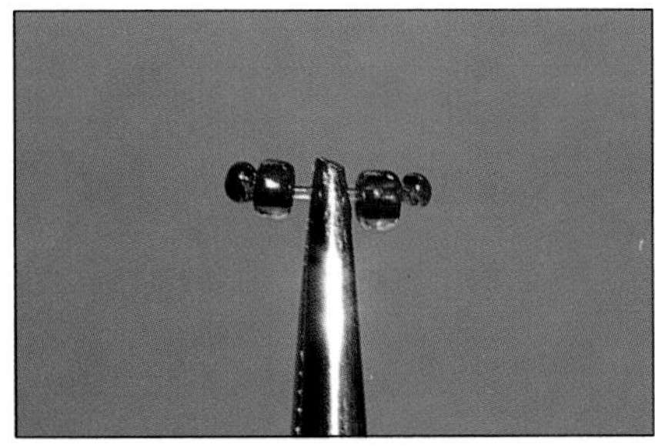

3. Finished glass bead eyes for the damsel.

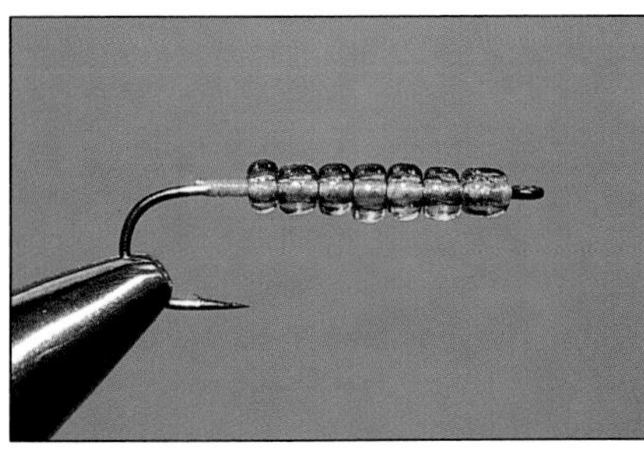

4. Flatten the barb on a size 12 Aberdeen hook. Start at the rear of the hook above the barb and tie in the thread. Cover the shank to the eye, half hitch twice and trim thread. Remove the hook and slide on 5 to 7 beads for the body and place the hook back into the vise.

5. Tie in the thread behind the beads. Tie in a sparse amount of marabou plumes for the tail and trim the butt leaving a small tuft. Push all the beads back slightly against the tuft and wrap the thread forward with two wraps between each bead. Tie off the thread at the eye and trim to complete the body and tail.

6. Remove the hook from the vise and use a pair of wire cutters to cut off the hook at the bend.

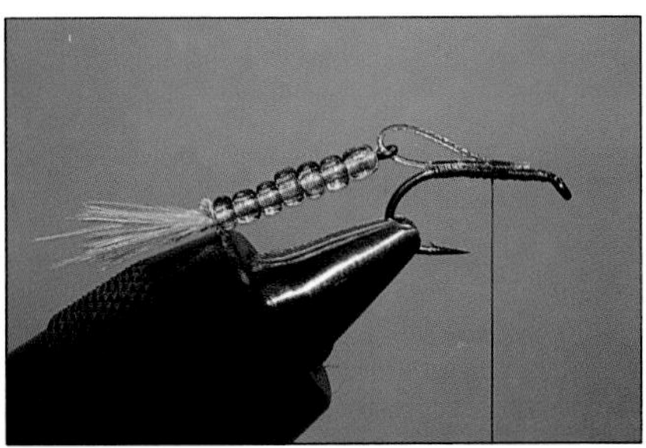

7. For the thorax, place a new hook into the vise and wrap the shank with a thread base. Use a one-inch-long piece of 12-pound mono to size up the loop connection for the body. The loop should barely extend past the bend of the hook. Flatten the arms of the mono and secure one arm of the mono onto the shank with tight thread wraps. Thread the loose arm of the mono through the eye of the Aberdeen hook and secure the second arm to the hook shank. Cement the thread wraps.

8. For the wingcase, secure the marabou plumes on top of the shank with the butts reaching the connection to the body and the tips extending forward past the hook eye (tips will be folded back over the top and should reach almost to the body).

9. Attach glass bead eyes about two hook eye lengths back from the hook's eye, using a figure-eight wrap over the mono stem and around the hook shank to secure the bead eyes. Start the thread at the hook's eye and apply dubbing material. Dub the head region and use figure-eight wraps of dubbing around the bead eyes.

10. At the thorax region tie in 6 to 8 guinea fibers for the legs on each side of the thorax. Complete the dubbing on the thorax and pull the marabou tips over the top for the wingcase. Secure the marabou with several thread wraps and half hitches.

## Joe's Sand Lance

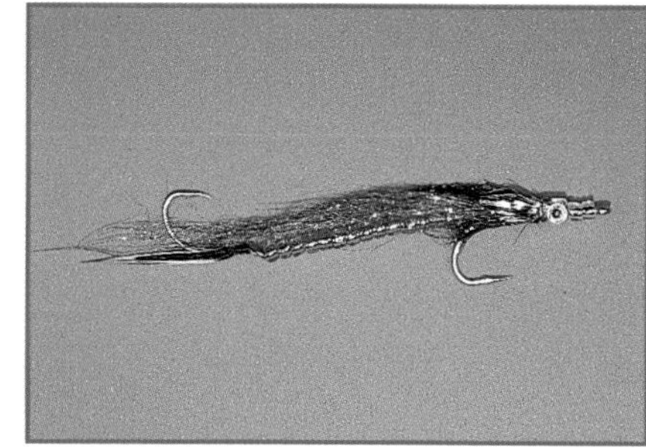

One of the many marine baitfishes widely distributed throughout the Pacific Ocean is the slender, eel-like fish, the Pacific sand lance (*Ammodytes hexapterus*). Also known as the candlefish or needlefish, they are sometimes found in large schools stemming tidal currents in channels, or burrowing themselves completely into the sand. They are a primary food source for both open-water and bottom-dwelling species such as salmon, lingcod, and halibut. Sand lances can obtain lengths up to eight inches but are commonly three to six inches long.

Joe's Sand Lance features beads threaded on a nylon-coated wire for a long baitfish profile. In 1995, Lee Clark was the first to introduce me to threading beads on a length of line. Although Lee uses monofilament, I find the stainless steel, nylon-coated wire to be easier to work with because of its smaller diameter and the use of the crimping sleeves as opposed to knots (see Assassin tying steps page 32).

The wire is looped through a trailer hook which can be tied with or without a tail. The trailer hook is optional, but recommended, for salmon which often short strike the fly without grabbing the main hook. When the beads have been threaded onto the wire, add a spot of Marine Goop to the front of the beads. This will prevent the beads from sliding which can scrape off the inside finish or cause the beads to shatter if they hit each other. Threading beads on nylon-coated wire is more effective than hunting for long streamer hooks which do not accommodate all beads because of their large wire diameter or the difficulty in maneuvering beads around their bend.

Joe's Sand Lance might serve as a successful pattern in the Atlantic waters where its relative, the sand eel, is a favorite prey of many coastal saltwater species, including the striper and bluefish.

## Joe's Sand Lance (aquamarine)

***Hook:*** Daiichi 2546, sizes 1/0-4; Daiichi 2556, sizes 2-6 for trailer hook

***Thread:*** Black 6/0 for tail, Kevlar to secure wire on front hook, and fine Translucent Thread to finish

***Tail:*** On trailer hook four to six badger hackle tips, notch out tip of feather to form forked tail

***Body:*** Fifteen aquamarine or diamond (sl) beads, large, threaded on 18-pound, nylon-coated, stainless steel American Fishing Wire, 7 inches long and looped in half through trailer hook

***Snout/Head:*** Two crystal (ir) beads, large; one crystal (ir) bead, x-large

***Wing:*** River green Lite Brite

***Topping:*** Dark olive Lite Brite

***Cheeks:*** Silver Flashabou

***Eyes:*** Temple Fork Lazer Eyes, small, glued on with Quick Gel Super Glue

**Note:** This pattern is 3 to 4 inches in length

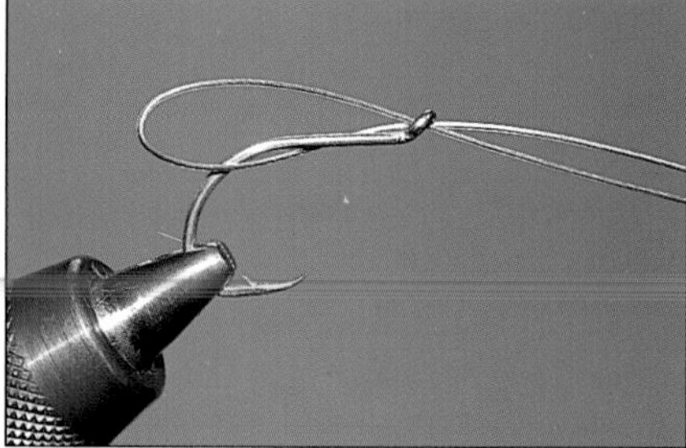

1. Place the trailer hook in the vise. Use seven inches of wire looped in half and pass the tags ends first through the back of the up-turned eye; draw the loop over the hook point and pull tight.

2. Tie in the thread behind the eye and wrap a thread base covering the shank. Select six badger hackles for the tail. Lay three hackles on top of each other and tie in on one side of the trailer hook with the shiny side facing you. Repeat on the other side of the hook with the remaining three badger hackles. Snip out the tips of the badger hackles to form a forked tail.

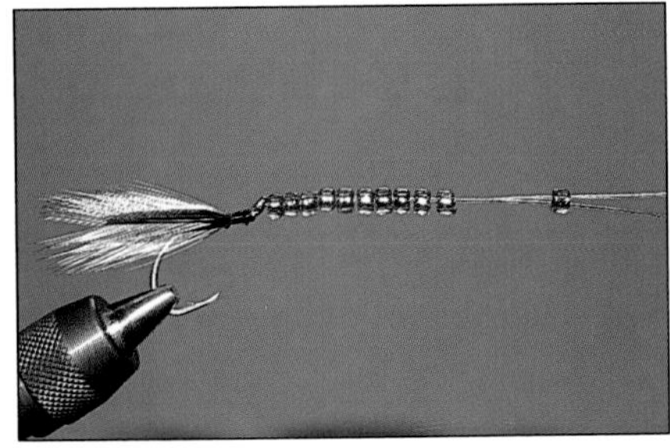

3. Thread 12 to 15 large beads onto the wire (it may be easier to do this off the vise).

4. Apply a small amount of Marine Goop ahead of the front bead (the Goop is very malleable without sticking to your fingers, I like to form a cone shape in front of the bead). This prevents the beads from sliding on the wire which makes them more vulnerable to breaking. I recommend allowing the glue to harden overnight, you might want to do a series of these and finish the flies on the following day.

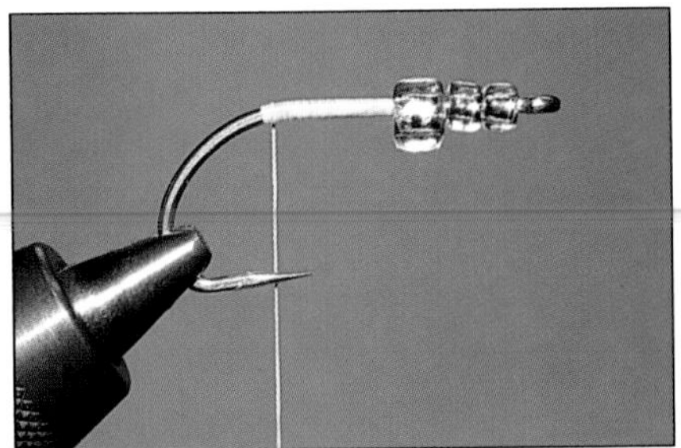

5. Thread two large beads and one x-large bead onto the hook and place it in the vise. Tie in the Kevlar thread behind the beads and cover the shank with tight wraps to the bend and back.

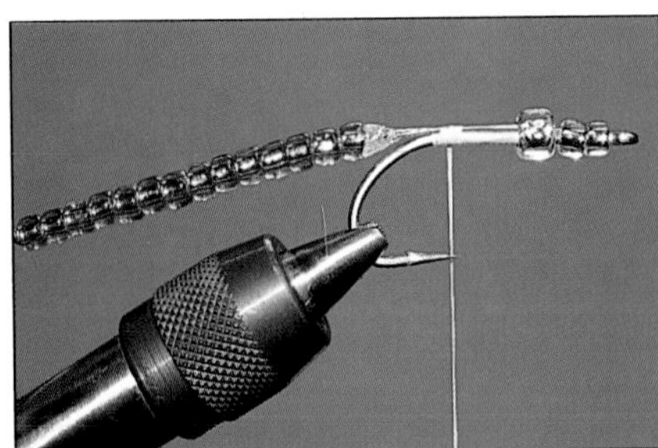

6. Size the length of the wire from the body so the glue spot is at the bend of the hook. Cut excess wire and secure the wire from the body atop the hook with tight wraps down to the bend and back. Make certain the trailer hook is riding up. As an option, Super Glue the thread wraps.

7. Tie in the Translucent Thread and secure the underwing, wing, and beard. Tie in the cheeks and half hitch the thread several times to finish.

8. Glue on the eyes to the sides of the x-large bead.

9. After the glue has dried, immerse the fly in hot water to shape the body.

## The Assassin

A vibrant tail of flashy beads does wonders for a bushy bucktail fly whether it's for saltwater or large freshwater predators. The Assassin was my first saltwater pattern, tied about one year ago as a general baitfish pattern. I wish I had had the privilege of delivering the first cast over lurking predators as one of my angling partners did when he took the prototypes of the Assassin to Baja Mexico. The Assassin scored on more than a dozen saltwater species, and the beads held up to the punishment of the crushing jaws of broomtail grouper and the needle teeth of barracuda. Since then I have added to the list by taking striped bass and Pacific rockfish species.

The wire and crimping sleeve help design the bulk of the pattern (because of the ease of forming a tail and bead body). By forming a loop through the crimping sleeve, you can firmly attach a tail by inserting the fibers into the loop and drawing the crimping sleeve taut. Rubber hackle or Krystal Flash also work well for the tail. Another approach for tying on the tail is to tie the material directly onto the crimping sleeve after it is flattened. If your vise is set up with jaws for large hooks, the crimping sleeve will hold in the jaws while you secure the material into place. Next you are ready to add beads to any length you desire using two or three sizes for a tapered body or alternating different colors for a two-tone effect.

For freshwater predators such as largemouth bass, striped bass, pike, etc., you might consider the wide gap stinger hook. For large trout I use a similar version with a trailer hook called the Razzma-Tazz Minnow (refer to the fly plates on page 48).

### The Assassin (herring)

***Hook:*** Daiichi 2546, standard saltwater hook, size 3/0-1/0
***Thread:*** Kevlar, tan
***Tail:*** Light blue pearlescent saltwater Flashabou inserted into wire loop with crimping sleeve drawn tight
***Body:*** Twelve diamond (sl) beads, large; six diamond (sl) beads, x-large, threaded on 40-pound, nylon-coated, stainless steel American Fishing Wire, 7 inches long and looped in half through a #3 crimping sleeve
***Snout/Head:*** Two diamond (sl) beads, x-large on 3/0 hook; use two large beads and one x-large bead on smaller hooks
***Wing:*** Blue bucktail
***Topping:*** Green bucktail or Super Hair
***Throat:*** White Bucktail
***Gills:*** Hot red bucktail
***Eyes:*** Temple Fork Lazer Eyes or white audible eyes, glued with Marine Goop
**Note:** This pattern is 5 to 6 inches in length.

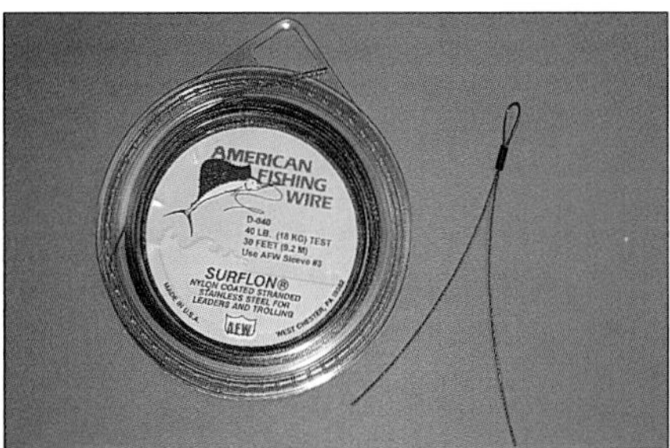


1. Cut a length of wire to seven inches long and loop in half. Insert the tag ends into a #3 crimping sleeve and pull the wire through until there is a small loop.

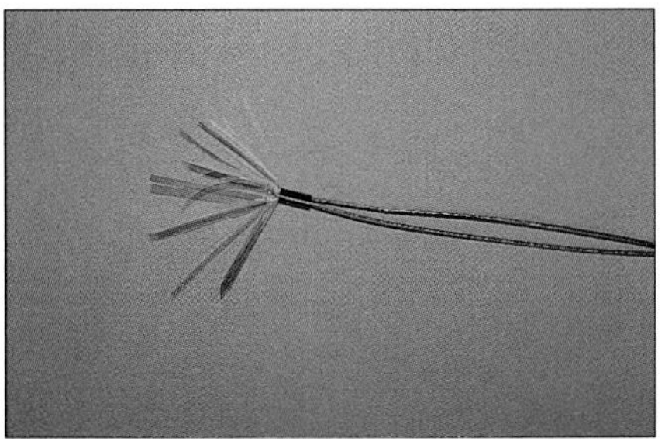

2. Insert the Flashabou into the wire loop and pull the wire taut through the crimping sleeve to secure the Flashabou tightly. Use a pair of pliers to flatten the crimping sleeve into place.

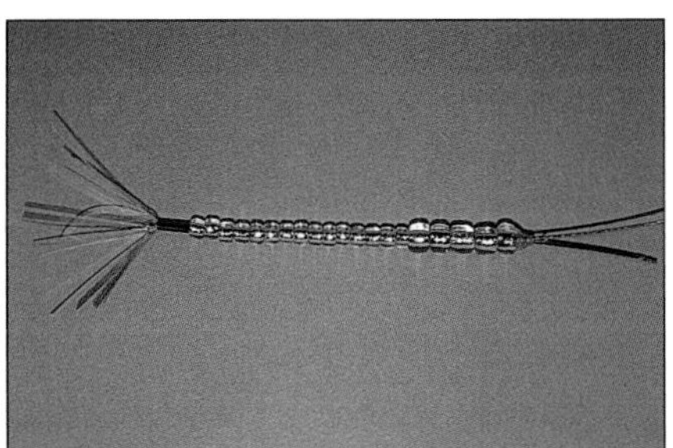

3. Thread the beads onto the wire to form the body. Add a spot of Marine Goop at the front of the beads.

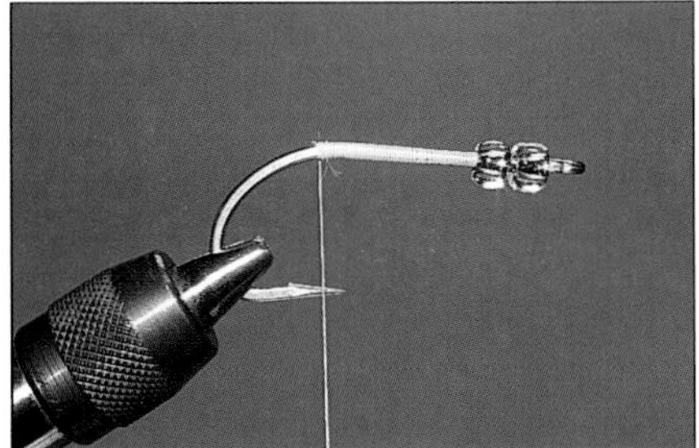

4. Thread two x-large beads onto the hook and place it in the vise. Tie in the Kevlar thread behind the beads and cover the shank with tight wraps to the bend.

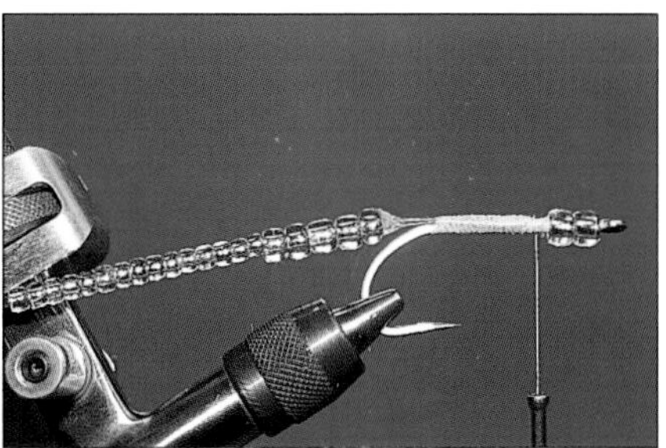

5. Size the length of the wire from the body so the glue spot is at the bend of the hook. Cut excess wire and secure the wire from the body atop the hook with tight wraps down to the bend and back. Make certain the trailer hook is riding up. As an option, Super Glue the thread wraps.

6. Tie in the Translucent Thread behind the beads. Rotate the fly upside down and tie on the belly material. Return the fly to the upright position and tie in the underwing, wing, and topping.

7. For the gills, tie in red bucktail on each side of the head (fibers are about half an inch long). Tie off the thread with multiple wraps and half hitches. Use Marine Goop and add a ring of glue all the way around the head behind the beads. Seat the eyes firmly into the Marine Goop to complete.

# Imitations of the Naturals

(Suggestive to Realistic)

| | | |
|---|---|---|
| **Mayflies** (1-18) | **Midges, Mosquitoes, Cranefly** (46-60) | **Worms, Leeches** (72-76) |
| **Stoneflies** (19-24) | **Damselflies, Dragonfly** (61-64) | **Terrestrials** (77-78) |
| **Caddisflies** (25-45) | **Crustaceans** (65-71) | **Fish Spawn** (79-81) |

A smorgasbord of trout delicacies, the flies in this chapter are arranged by the species they imitate. The insect groups are not strictly composed of nymph patterns, but also contain emergers and dry flies. In addition to trout, many of these patterns are well-suited for panfish, bass, white-fish, and steelhead. For example, the Glass Hare Worm is an excellent pattern for bass which fishes weedless and takes only seconds to tie. If you haven't already viewed the tying steps, spend some time going through Chapters 2, 3, and 4 to become familiar with the design of these patterns.

## Mayflies

**1. All-Purpose Seed Bead Nymph (black)**
***Hook:*** Daiichi 1270, 1273, sizes 12-14
***Thread:*** Black 8/0
***Body:*** Four or five black beads, small
***Tail:*** Gray partridge fibers
***Wingcase:*** Gray partridge fibers
***Thorax:*** Black hare dubbing
***Legs:*** Tips from wingcase splayed back

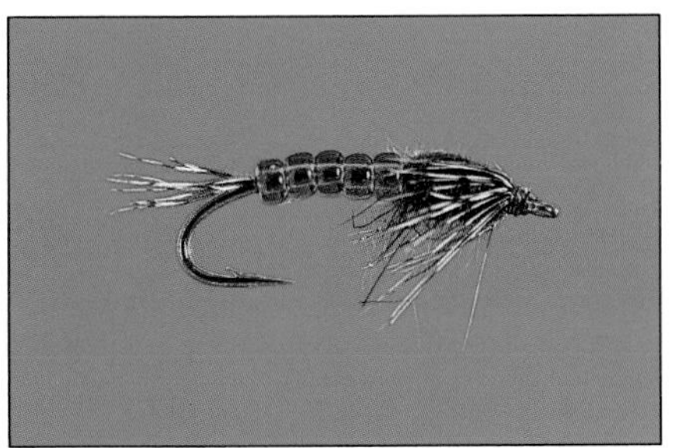

**2. A.P. Seed Bead Nymph (brown)**
***Hook:*** Daiichi 1270, 1273, sizes 12-14
***Thread:*** Brown 8/0
***Body:*** Four or five root beer (tr) beads, small
***Tail:*** Brown partridge fibers
***Wingcase:*** Brown partridge fibers
***Thorax:*** Brown hare dubbing
***Legs:*** Tips from wingcase splayed back

**3. A.P. Seed Bead Nymph (gray)**
***Hook:*** Daiichi 1270, 1273, sizes 12-14
***Thread:*** Gray 8/0
***Body:*** Four or five gunmetal (m) beads, small
***Tail:*** Gray partridge fibers
***Wingcase:*** Gray partridge fibers
***Thorax:*** Gray hare dubbing
***Legs:*** Tips from wingcase splayed back

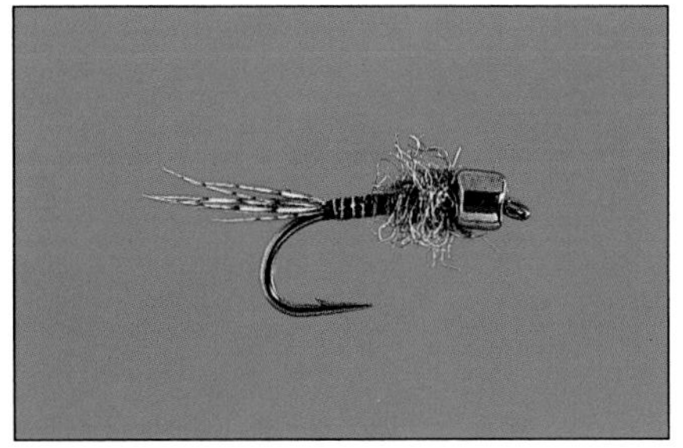

**4. Blue-wing Olive Glass Bead Head**
***Originator:*** Joe Warren
***Hook:*** Daiichi 1560, sizes 16-18
***Thread:*** Black 8/0
***Head:*** Blue dun (tr) bead, small
***Tail:*** Gray partridge fibers
***Body:*** Stripped peacock herl
***Thorax:*** Dark olive fur dubbing

**5. Cripple Bead (*Baetis*)**
***Originator and Tier:*** Bill Myers
***Hook:*** Tiemco 900BL, Daiichi 1190, sizes 14-16
***Thread:*** Rusty dun 8/0
***Air Bubble:*** Crystal (ir) bead, small
***Body:*** Pheasant tail fibers from tail
***Wing:*** Gray Z-lon
***Hackle:*** Dyed-green grizzly hackle

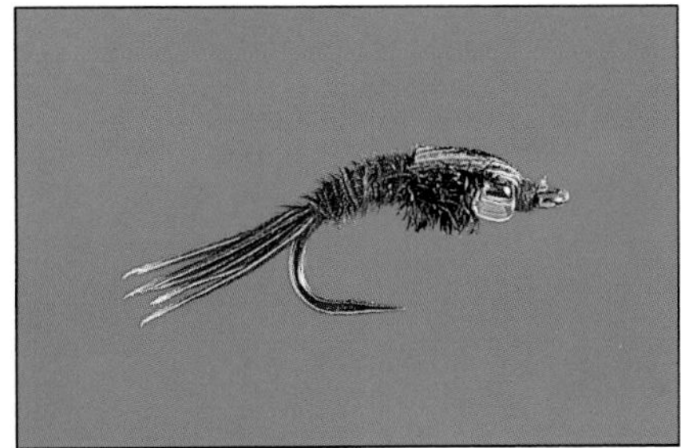

**6. D.B. Pheasant Tail**
***Tier:*** Dennis Brown
***Hook:*** Daiichi 1150, 1250, sizes 14-18
***Thread:*** Wine 6/0
***Head:*** Pearl (ir) Killer Caddis bead, small or "midge" size
***Tail:*** Pheasant tail fibers
***Ribbing:*** Fine gold wire
***Body:*** Pheasant tail fibers
***Wingcase:*** Lacquered pheasant tail fibers
***Thorax:*** Peacock herl

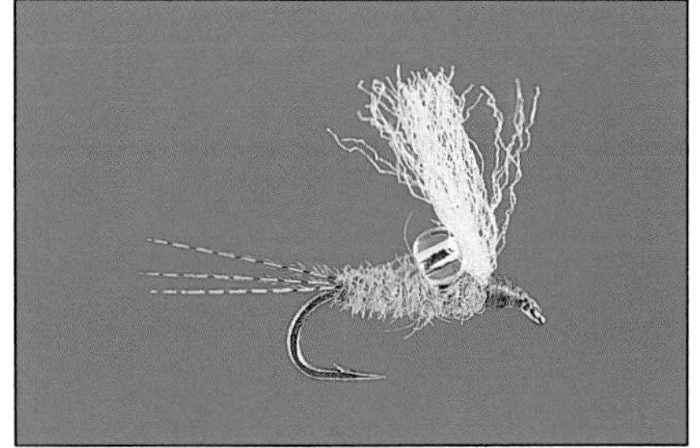

**7. Gas Bubble Bead Scuba Diving Olive**
***Originator and Tier:*** John Ciulla
***Hook:*** Daiichi 1180, size 18
***Thread:*** Olive 8/0
***Tail:*** Wood duck flank fibers
***Body:*** Olive rabbit dubbing
***Gas Bubble:*** Gas Bubble Bead
***Wing:*** Light gray poly yarn

**8. Glass Hare's Ear**
***Tier:*** Bill Black
***Hook:*** Daiichi 1270, sizes 12-16
***Thread:*** At tail, color matches beads; finish with color to match dubbing, 6/0
***Body:*** Five gold (sl) beads, small
***Tail:*** Gray partridge fibers
***Thorax:*** Squirrel dubbing
***Wingcase:*** Oak mottled turkey
***Legs:*** Squirrel dubbing picked out

**9. Metallic Pheasant Tail Nymph**
***Hook:*** Daiichi 1270 or 1273, sizes 8-14
***Thread:*** Brown 6/0
***Body:*** Four or five brown or copper (m) beads, medium or small
***Tail:*** Pheasant tail fibers
***Wingcase:*** Pheasant tail fibers
***Thorax:*** Peacock herl
***Legs:*** Tips from wingcase splayed back

**10. Neutron Nymph**
***Originator and Tier:*** Dennis Brown
***Hook:*** Daiichi 1150, 1250 sizes 14-18
***Thread:*** Wine 6/0
***Body:*** Three gunmetal (m) Killer Caddis beads, small or midge
***Tail:*** Pheasant tail fibers
***Wingcase:*** Lacquered pheasant tail fibers
***Thorax:*** Peacock herl

**11. Pebble Bead Head Emerger (black)**
***Hook:*** Daiichi 1270 or 1273, sizes 10-16
***Thread:*** Black 8/0
***Head:*** Charcoal (m) bead, medium or small
***Tail:*** Gray partridge fibers
***Ribbing:*** Fine gold wire
***Body:*** Black hare dubbing
***Wingcase:*** Natural coastal deer hair
***Thorax:*** Black hare dubbing
***Wing:*** Tips from wingcase tied upright

**12. Pebble Bead Head Emerger (brown)**
***Hook:*** Daiichi 1270 or 1273, sizes 10-16
***Thread:*** Brown 8/0
***Head:*** Brown (m) bead, medium or small
***Tail:*** Brown partridge fibers
***Ribbing:*** Fine gold wire
***Body:*** Brown hare dubbing
***Wingcase:*** Dyed-brown coastal deer hair
***Thorax:*** Brown hare dubbing
***Wing:*** Tips from wingcase tied upright

**13. Pebble Bead Head Emerger (gray)**
***Hook:*** Daiichi 1270, 1273, sizes 10-16
***Thread:*** Gray 8/0
***Head:*** Steel (m) bead, medium or small
***Tail:*** Gray partridge fibers
***Ribbing:*** Fine gold wire
***Body:*** Gray hare dubbing
***Wingcase:*** Natural coastal deer hair
***Thorax:*** Gray hare dubbing
***Wing:*** Tips from wingcase tied upright

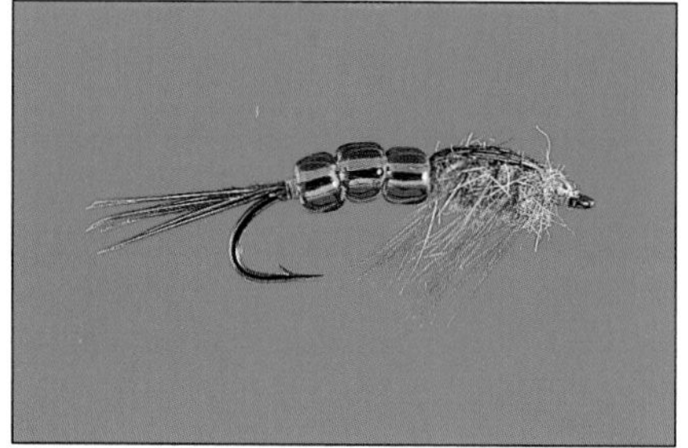

**14. Pebble Bead March Brown**
***Tier:*** Ken Tiffan
***Hook:*** Daiichi 1270, 1273, sizes 6-8
***Thread:*** Tan 6/0
***Body:*** Three root beer (sl) beads, large
***Tail:*** Pheasant tail fibers
***Wingcase:*** Pheasant tail fibers
***Legs:*** Brown hackle
***Thorax:*** Hare's ear mask dubbing

**15. Pebble Bead Olive Brown Nymph**
***Hook:*** Daiichi 1270, 1273, sizes 8-10
***Thread:*** Olive 6/0
***Body:*** Three or four brown (m) beads, medium
***Tail:*** Pheasant tail fibers
***Bead Dressing:*** Dyed-olive soft Chickabou wrapped twice between beads and trimmed short
***Wingcase:*** Pheasant tail fibers
***Thorax:*** Olive brown hare dubbing
***Legs:*** Dyed-olive soft Chickabou tips

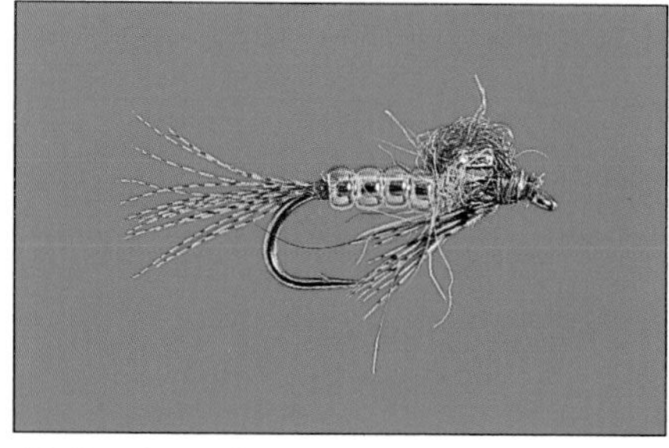

**16. Seed Bead *Callibaetis* Emerger**
***Hook:*** Daiichi 1560, sizes 12-14
***Thread:*** Olive 8/0
***Body:*** Four autumn (ir) beads, small
***Tail:*** Wood duck flank fibers
***Thorax:*** Olive hare's ear dubbing
***Air Bubble:*** Diamond (sl) bead, small
***Wingcase:*** Dark brown poly yarn
***Legs:*** Brown partridge fibers

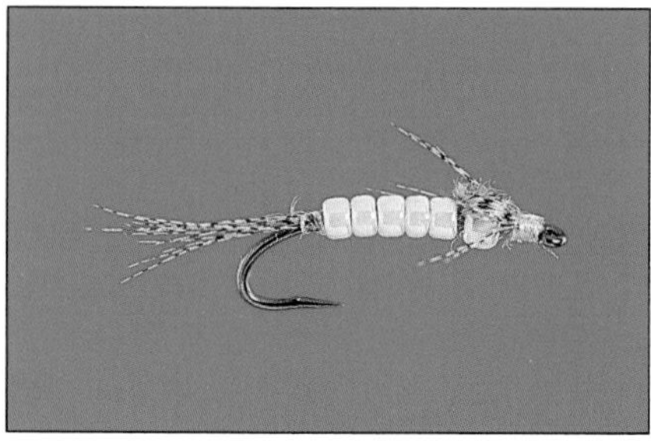

**17. Seed Bead Light Cahill**
***Hook:*** Daiichi 1270 or 1273, sizes 14-18
***Thread:*** White or cream 8/0
***Thorax:*** Chamois (p) bead, small
***Body:*** Five chamois or cream (p) beads, x-small
***Tail:*** Wood duck flank fibers
***Wingcase:*** Wood duck flank fibers
***Legs:*** Tips from wingcase splayed back

**18. Wiggle Hex**
***Hook:*** Daiichi 1530, sizes 2-6 for thoracic
***Thread:*** Brown 6/0
***Tail:*** Tan or natural ostrich herl, 3 strands
***Body:*** Four or five tan (tr) beads, large, threaded on 18-pound nylon-coated, stainless steel American Fishing Wire, 2.5 inches long, looped through a #2 crimping sleeve; use additional wire to form loop from thorax and make loop to loop connection.
***Bead Dressing:*** Sand and light brown Clark's Tying Yarn combed together
***Thorax:*** Golden brown hare dubbing
***Legs:*** Brown partridge fibers
***Wingcase:*** Lacquered turkey tail fibers
***Eyes:*** Mini lead barbells (4/32)
***Antennae:*** Natural goose biots
***Head:*** Golden brown hare dubbing

## Stoneflies

**19. D.B. Stimulator**
*Tier:* Dennis Brown
*Hook:* Daiichi 1270, sizes 12-16
*Thread:* Yellow 6/0
*Thorax:* Scarlet (ir) Killer Caddis bead, small
*Body:* Bright yellow dubbing
*Body Hackle:* Brown
*Wing:* Light elk hair
*Hackle:* Grizzly
*Thorax:* Bright orange dubbing

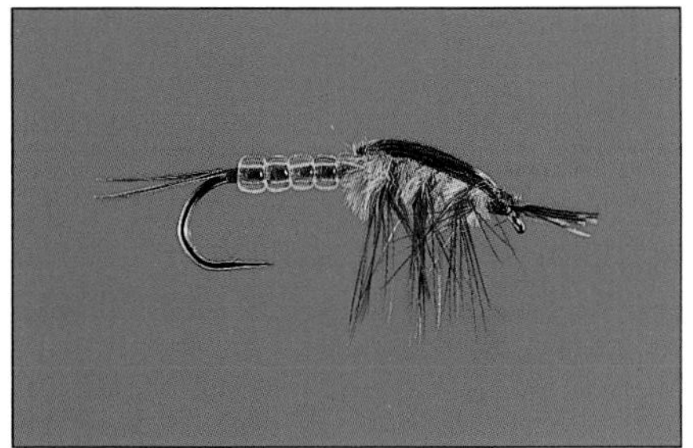

**20. Pebble Bead Golden Stone**
*Originator:* Joe Warren
*Hook:* Daiichi 1270, 1730, sizes 6-8
*Thread:* Brown 6/0
*Underbody:* Brown thread
*Body:* Four or five yellow (tr) beads, medium
*Tail:* Lacquered pheasant tail fibers
*Weight (optional):* .020" or .025" diameter lead wraps at thorax
*Antennae:* Lacquered pheasant tail fibers, two-thirds length of tail
*Wingcase:* Mottled turkey quill
*Legs:* Brown hackle
*Thorax:* Golden yellow ostrich herl

**21. Pebble Bead Stonefly (brown)**
*Originator:* Joe Warren
*Hook:* Daiichi 1270, 1730, sizes 2-4
*Thread:* Brown 6/0
*Underbody:* Brown yarn
*Body:* Five brown/pearl (sl) beads, large
*Tail:* Brown goose biots
*Weight (optional):* .025" or .030" diameter lead wraps at thorax
*Antennae:* Brown rubber legs
*Wingcase:* Mottle turkey quill
*Legs:* Brown hackle
*Thorax:* Brown dubbing or chenille

**22. Pebble Bead Stonefly (dark)**
*Hook:* Daiichi 1270, 1730, sizes 2-4
*Thread:* Black 6/0
*Underbody:* Black yarn, single strand
*Body:* Five black beads, large
*Tail:* Black goose biots
*Weight (optional):* .025" or .030" diameter lead wraps at thorax
*Antennae:* Brown rubber legs
*Wingcase:* Dark peacock quill
*Legs:* Grizzly hackle
*Thorax:* Black dubbing or chenille

**23. Phil's Red Glass Stone**
*Originator and Tier:* Phil Brummet
*Hook:* Daiichi 1270, sizes 4-6
*Thread:* Black 6/0
*Body:* Four dark red (tr) beads, large
*Bead Dressing:* Black and red Angora mixed 50/50
*Wingcase:* Black 1/4 inch scud back
*Thorax:* Black and red Angora mixed 50/50
*Legs:* Red dyed grizzly hackle
*Eyes:* Lead or non-toxic barbell eyes

**24. Seed Bead Little Yellow Sally**
*Hook:* Daiichi 1270, 1273, sizes 10-14
*Thread:* Brown 8/0
*Body:* Five golden yellow (ic) beads, small
*Tail:* Brown partridge fibers
*Wingcase:* Dark brown partridge fibers
*Thorax:* Antique gold fur dubbing
*Legs:* Tips from wingcase splayed back

## Caddisflies

**25. Bead Butt Caddis**
*Originator and Tier:* Dennis Brown
*Hook:* Daiichi 1180, sizes 12-16
*Egg Sac:* Caddis green (ir) Killer Caddis bead, small
*Body:* Medium brown dubbing
*Hackle:* Brown
*Wing:* Light elk hair

**26. Chamois Caseless Caddis**
*Originator:* Joe Warren
*Hook:* Daiichi 1150, 1250, sizes 10-14
*Thread:* Black 8/0
*Body:* Five chamois (p) beads, small
*Butt:* Black hare dubbing
*Bead Dressing:* Black Clark's Tying Yarn
*Head:* Black ostrich herl

**27. Clark's Tied Down Caddis**
*Tier:* Lee Clark
*Hook:* Mustad 9672, Daiichi 1720, size 8
*Thread:* Orange 6/0
*Body:* Five orange (sl) beads, large
*Tail:* Red Clark's Tying Yarn
*Bead Dressing:* Brown hackle
*Back:* Deer hair, strengthen with Dave's Flexament

**28. Emerging Carbonated Caddis**
***Hook:*** Daiichi 1150, 1250, sizes 12-16
***Thread:*** Olive 8/0
***Air Bubble:*** Diamond (sl) bead, small or medium
***Body:*** Fur dubbing, color to match natural
***Wing:*** Brown partridge fibers
***Head:*** Brown, black, or olive ostrich herl

**29. Gas Bubble Pupa**
***Originator and Tier:*** John Ciulla
***Hook:*** Partridge K2B, Daiichi 1150, size to match natural
***Thread:*** Color to match head of natural
***Gas Bubbles:*** Gas Bubble Beads with fur dubbing between the beads, color to match natural
***Wings:*** Ostrich herl, color to match natural
***Color:*** Partridge, grouse or duck flank fibers, color to match legs of natural

**30. Glass Emerger (brown)**
***Originator and Tier:*** Bill Black
***Hook:*** Daiichi 1710, sizes 12-14
***Thread:*** At tail, color matches beads; finish with color to match dubbing, 6/0
***Body:*** Four brown/pearl (sl) beads, small
***Tail:*** Gray-dyed Polar Aire fibers
***Legs:*** Mallard-dyed wood duck
***Wing:*** Dark deer hair
***Thorax:*** Dark hare's ear brown Squirrel Brite Dubbing

**31. Glass Emerger (gold)**
***Tier:*** Bill Black
***Hook:*** Daiichi 1710, sizes 12-14
***Thread:*** At tail, color matches bead; finish with color to match dubbing, 6/0
***Body:*** Four gold/pearl (sl) beads, small
***Tail:*** Gray-dyed Polar Aire fibers
***Legs:*** Mallard dyed wood duck
***Wing:*** Dark deer hair
***Thorax:*** Dark hare's ear brown Squirrel Brite Dubbing

**32. Green Rock Bead**
***Originator and Tier:*** Bill Myers
***Hook:*** Tiemco 200R, Daiichi 1270, size 14
***Thread:*** Black 8/0
***Body:*** Seven peacock (tr) beads, small
***Head:*** Black rabbit dubbing

**33. Joe's Green Rock Larva**
***Originator:*** Joe Warren
***Hook:*** Daiichi 1155, sizes 12-16
***Thread:*** Olive 8/0
***Body:*** Four or five light green (ir) beads, small
***Tail:*** Green Clark's Tying Yarn, short and sparse
***Bead Dressing:*** Green Clark's Tying Yarn, very sparse
***Legs:*** Brown Clark's Tying Yarn, slightly longer lengths than bead dressing
***Head:*** Olive brown fur dubbing

**34. Killer Caddis (caddis green)**
***Originator and Tier:*** Dennis Brown
***Hook:*** Daiichi 1250, sizes 12-18
***Thread:*** Chartreuse at butt, wine to finish, 6/0
***Body:*** Three or four caddis green (ir) Killer Caddis beads, small or midge
***Butt:*** Antron dubbing, color of beads
***Head:*** Black natural fur dubbing
***Note:*** Additional bead colors: gunmetal, amber, peacock, scarlet, or chamois

**35. Killer Caddis (olive)**
***Tier:*** Dennis Brown
***Hook:*** Daiichi 1250, sizes 12-18
***Thread:*** Chartreuse at butt, wine to finish, 6/0
***Body:*** Three or four olive (m) Killer Caddis beads, small or midge
***Butt:*** Antron dubbing, color of beads
***Head:*** Black natural fur dubbing

**36. Pearl Cased Caddis**
***Originator and Tier:*** Bill Black
***Hook:*** Daiichi 1270, sizes 8-10
***Thread:*** Black 6/0
***Caddis Body:*** Sulphur (p) bead, medium
***Ribbing:*** Fine gold wire counter-wrapped
***Body Case:*** Fine lead wraps for weight, rainbow Lite Brite dubbed and plucked out with 3-4 peacock herls twisted and palmered over dubbing

**37. Pettis' Gold Bead Pulsating Caddis (*Brachycentrus*)**
***Originator and Tier:*** Jim Pettis
***Hook:*** Tiemco 2487, Daiichi 1130, sizes 14-16
***Thread:*** Olive 6/0, prewaxed
***Bead Head:*** Gold, medium or small
***Body:*** Three to four deep green (sl) beads, small
***Bead Dressing:*** Olive brown Buggy Nymph Dubbing
***Legs:*** Wood duck flank fibers
***Thorax:*** Dark brown Buggy Nymph Dubbing

**38. Pettis' Gold Bead Pulsating Caddis (*Hydropsyche*)**
***Tier:*** Jim Pettis
***Hook:*** Tiemco 2457, Daiichi 1250, sizes 12-16
***Thread:*** Olive 6/0, prewaxed
***Bead Head:*** Gold, medium or small
***Body:*** Three to five light orange (sl) beads, small
***Bead Dressing:*** Lava brown Buggy Nymph Dubbing
***Legs:*** Wood duck flank fibers
***Thorax:*** Dark brown Buggy Nymph Dubbing

**39. Pettis' Pulsating Caddis (*Brachycentrus*)**
***Originator and Tier:*** Jim Pettis
***Hook:*** Tiemco 2487, Daiichi 1130, sizes 14-16
***Thread:*** Olive 6/0, prewaxed
***Body:*** Four to five deep green (sl) beads, small
***Bead Dressing:*** Olive brown Buggy Nymph Dubbing
***Legs:*** Wood duck flank fibers
***Head:*** Dark brown Buggy Nymph dubbing

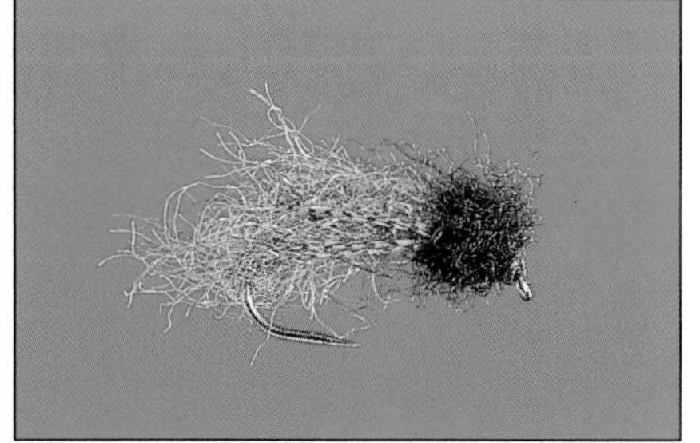

**40. Pettis' Pulsating Caddis (*Hydropsyche*)**
***Tier:*** Jim Pettis
***Hook:*** Tiemco 2457, Daiichi 1250, sizes 12-16
***Thread:*** Olive 6/0, prewaxed
***Body:*** Four to six orange (sl) beads, small
***Bead Dressing:*** Lava brown Buggy Nymph Dubbing
***Legs:*** Wood duck flank fibers
***Head:*** Dark brown Buggy Nymph Dubbing

**41. Pettis' Pulsating Caddis Emerger (*Brachycentrus*)**
***Originator and Tier:*** Jim Pettis
***Hook:*** Tiemco 200, Daiichi 1270, size 16
***Thread:*** Olive 6/0, prewaxed
***Body:*** Three deep green (sl) beads, small
***Bead Dressing:*** Olive brown Buggy Nymph Dubbing
***Split:*** Dark olive brown marabou
***Upper Body:*** Light hare's ear Buggy Nymph Dubbing
***Legs:*** Wood duck fibers
***Wings:*** Medium to dark gray deer hair

**42. Pettis' Pulsating Caddis Emerger (*Hydropsyche*)**
***Tier:*** Jim Pettis
***Hook:*** Tiemco 200, Daiichi 1270, size 16
***Thread:*** Olive 6/0, prewaxed
***Body:*** Three light orange (sl) beads, small
***Bead Dressing:*** Lava brown Buggy Nymph dubbing
***Split:*** Dark olive brown marabou
***Upper Body:*** Pale olive yellow Scintilla Multi-Purpose Dubbing
***Legs:*** Wood duck fibers
***Wings:*** Light tan elk hair

**43. Seed Bead Caddis Larva, Heavy**
***Originator:*** Joe Warren
***Hook:*** Daiichi 1270, 1710, sizes 12-16
***Thread:*** Olive 6/0
***Bead Head:*** Gold (1/8)
***Body:*** Five light green (ir) beads, small
***Legs:*** Brown partridge fibers, beard style
***Thorax:*** Peacock herl

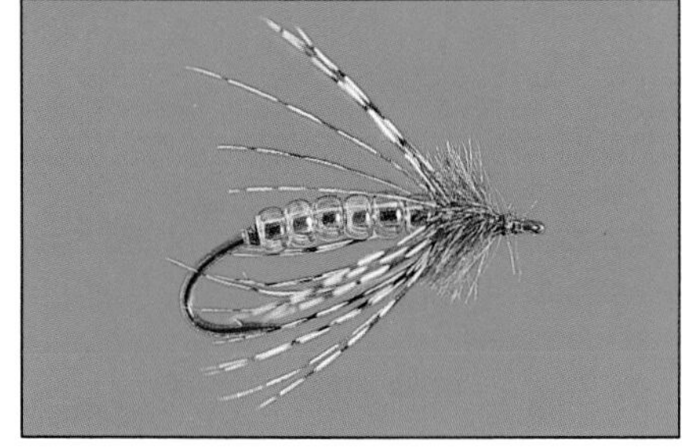

**44. Seed Bead Caddis Pupa**
***Hook:*** Daiichi 1270, sizes 12-16
***Thread:*** Olive 8/0
***Body:*** Six caddis green (ir) beads, small
***Hackle:*** Brown partridge
***Head:*** Brown ostrich herl

**45. Seed Bead Sparkle Pupa**
***Hook:*** Daiichi 1155, sizes 12-16
***Thread:*** Olive 8/0
***Body:*** Three or four olive/pearl (sl) beads, small; sand Clark's Tying Yarn tied top and bottom of hook at bend and pulled over beads
***Wing:*** Brown ostrich herl
***Legs:*** Brown partridge fibers
***Head:*** Olive brown hare dubbing

## Midges, Mosquito, Cranefly

**46. D.B. Bloodworm**
***Originator and Tier:*** Dennis Brown
***Hook:*** Daiichi 1270, sizes 14-16
***Thread:*** Black 6/0
***Body:*** Two scarlet (tr) beads, midge; one scarlet (ir) bead, small; three scarlet (tr) beads, midge
***Butt:*** Brown Rainy's Mini Mohair yarn
***Bead Dressing:*** Brown Rainy's Mini Mohair yarn
***Head:*** Peacock herl

**47. D.B. Bloodworm**
***Tier:*** Dennis Brown
***Hook:*** Daiichi 1270, sizes 18-20
***Thread:*** Black 6/0
***Body:*** Four or five scarlet (tr) Killer Caddis beads, midge
***Butt:*** Brown Rainy's Mini Mohair yarn
***Bead Dressing:*** Brown Rainy's Mini Mohair yarn
***Head:*** Peacock herl

**48. D.B. Midge**
***Originator and Tier:*** Dennis Brown
***Hook:*** Daiichi 1180, sizes 18-20
***Thread:*** Wine 6/0
***Body:*** Two gunmetal (m) Killer Caddis beads, midge
***Tail:*** Antron yarn
***Body Hackle:*** Grizzly palmered at tail and between the beads

**49. Double Ender (black)**
***Originator and Tier:*** Henry Hoffman
***Hook:*** Mustad 3906B, Daiichi 1560, sizes 10-16
***Thread:*** Black 8/0
***Head:*** Diamond (sl) bead, medium
***Tail:*** White Chickabou tip fibers
***Ribbing:*** Fine copper wire
***Body:*** Black Super Floss
***Gills:*** White Chickabou tip fibers

**50. Double Ender (chartreuse)**
***Tier:*** Henry Hoffman
***Hook:*** Mustad 3906B, Daiichi 1560, sizes 10-16
***Thread:*** Chartreuse 8/0
***Head:*** Light green (ir) bead, small
***Tail:*** White Chickabou tip fibers
***Ribbing:*** Fine copper wire
***Body:*** Chartreuse Super Floss
***Gills:*** White Chickabou tip fibers

**51. Double Ender (olive)**
***Tier:*** Henry Hoffman
***Hook:*** Mustad 3906B, Daiichi 1560, sizes 10-16
***Thread:*** Olive 8/0
***Head:*** Gold (sl) bead, medium
***Tail:*** White Chickabou tip fibers
***Ribbing:*** Fine copper wire
***Body:*** Olive Super Floss
***Gills:*** White Chickabou tip fibers

**52. Glass Palomino**
***Hook:*** Daiichi 1510, sizes 16-18
***Thread:*** Color to match body
***Thorax:*** Blue, black, brown, or red (m, tr) bead, small
***Body:*** Black, brown, or red Micro Ultra Chenille (1mm)
***Wingcase:*** White poly yarn fibers
***Antennae:*** Fibers from wingcase

**53. Glass Serendipity**
***Hook:*** Daiichi 1273, sizes 16-18
***Thread:*** Color to match beads
***Body:*** Five or four red (tr), root beer (tr) or black beads, x-small
***Wingcase:*** Trimmed deer hair

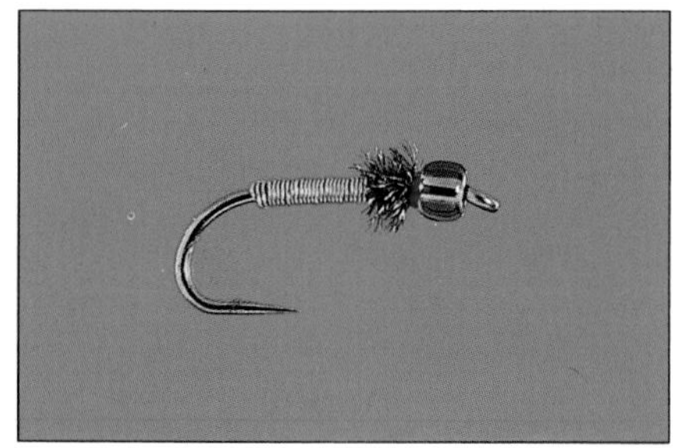

**54. Glassie Brassie**
***Hook:*** Daiichi 1560, sizes 14-18
***Thread:*** Olive 8/0
***Thorax:*** Root beer (sl) bead, small
***Body:*** Small copper wire
***Head:*** Peacock herl



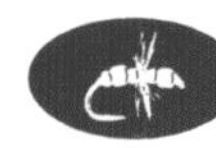

**55. Mystic Midge**
***Hook:*** Daiichi 1273, sizes 16-20
***Thread:*** Olive 8/0
***Body:*** Four to six root beer (tr), red (tr) or black beads, x-small
***Tail:*** Clear poly yarn
***Wingcase (optional):*** gray hackle fibers
***Thorax:*** Peacock herl
***Antennae:*** Clear poly yarn

**56. Peacock Seed Bead Midge**
***Originator and Tier:*** Chuck Cameron
***Hook:*** Tiemco 200R, Daiichi 1273, sizes 10-12
***Thread:*** Black 6/0
***Body:*** Five or six peacock (tr) beads, small
***Tail:*** Peacock sword or tips, 2 strands of pearl Krystal Flash on each side
***Bead Dressing:*** Peacock herl
***Head:*** White ostrich herl

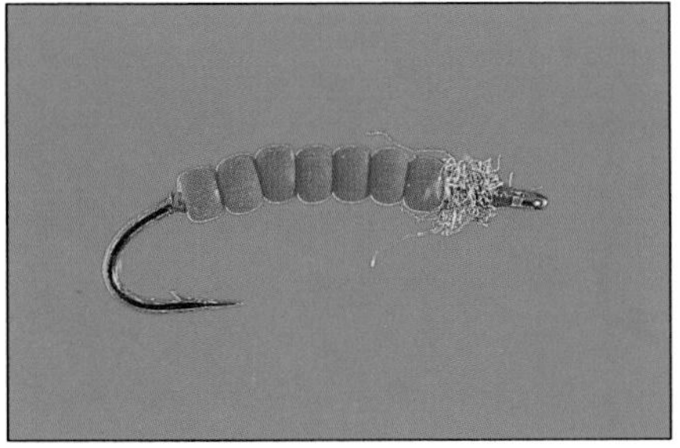

**57. Seed Bead Blood Larva**
***Hook:*** Daiichi 1273, sizes 12-20
***Thread:*** Brown 8/0
***Body:*** Six or seven red frost or translucent beads, small or x-small
***Head:*** Brown Squirrel Brite Dubbing; head should be smaller than body

**58. Seed Bead Midge Pupa**
***Hook:*** Daiichi 1150, sizes 12-14
***Thread:*** Black 8/0
***Body:*** Four or 5 root beer (sl), caddis green (tr), or black beads; small
***Tail:*** Black poly yarn fibers; tip of black goose biot over top
***Head:*** Black ostrich herl

**59. Glass Mosquito Larva**
***Hook:*** Daiichi 1560, sizes 12-16
***Thread:*** Olive 8/0
***Head:*** Peacock (tr) bead, small
***Tail:*** Grizzly hackle fibers
***Body:*** Dark moose hair fiber ribbed with light moose hair fiber
***Antennae:*** Great gadwall flank fibers

**60. D.B. Cranefly Larva**
***Originator and Tier:*** Dennis Brown
***Hook:*** Daiichi 1870, sizes 6-8
***Thread:*** Black 3/0 mono cord
***Body:*** Six blueberry (tr) beads, medium; one root beer (sl) bead, large (optional)
***Butt:*** Gray Mohair
***Bead Dressing:*** Gray Mohair
***Head:*** Gray natural fur dubbing

## Damselflies, Dragonfly

**61. The Boogie Damsel**
***Hook:*** Daiichi 1530, sizes 10-12 for thoracic
***Thread:*** Light olive 8/0
***Body:*** Seven or eight light green, olive/pearl (tr or sl) or gold (sl) beads, small, threaded on a size 12 Aberdeen hook, cut off bend after completing body. Use 12-pound mono through Aberdeen hook eye to connect body to thorax
***Tail:*** Light olive marabou tip fibers
***Wingcase:*** Light olive marabou
***Thorax:*** Olive shade to suit, hare dubbing
***Legs:*** Dyed yellow or olive guinea
***Eyes:*** Burgundy (tr) or peacock green (tr) beads, small, mounted on 20-pound mono
***Head:*** Olive shade to suit, hare dubbing

**62. D.B. Damsel Nymph**
***Tier:*** Dennis Brown
***Hook:*** Daiichi 1270, sizes 6-10
***Thread:*** Olive or black mono cord
***Body:*** Five to seven olive (m) Killer Caddis beads, small
***Tail:*** Olive marabou
***Bead Dressing:*** Olive Rainy's Micro Mohair Yarn
***Eyes:*** Gunmetal (m) Killer Caddis beads, small
***Wingcase:*** Lacquered pheasant tail
***Thorax:*** Olive marabou

**63. Seed Bead Damsel**
***Originator:*** Joe Warren
***Hook:*** Daiichi 1270, 1770, sizes 10-12
***Thread:*** Light olive 8/0
***Body:*** Light green, olive/pearl (tr or sl) or gold (sl) beads, small
***Tail:*** Light olive marabou tip fibers
***Wingcase:*** Light olive marabou
***Thorax:*** Damsel olive hare dubbing
***Legs:*** Dyed yellow or olive guinea
***Eyes:*** Peacock green (tr) beads, x-small, mounted on 15-pound mono
***Head:*** Damsel olive hare dubbing

**64. Joe's Dragonfly Nymph**
***Originator:*** Joe Warren
***Hook:*** Daiichi 2340, sizes 4-8
***Thread:*** Olive 6/0
***Body:*** Five or six olive/pearl (sl) beads, large
***Tail:*** Olive marabou
***Bead Dressing:*** Gold and light brown Clark's Tying Yarn, half a strand of each and combed together
***Legs:*** Brown ringneck pheasant flank for hind legs, picked out dubbing for front legs
***Thorax:*** Olive brown hare dubbing
***Eyes:*** Dark green (tr) beads, small, mounted on 15-pound mono
***Wingcase:*** Dark turkey quill
***Head:*** Olive brown hare dubbing

## Crustaceans

**65. Joe's Sow Bug**
***Originator:*** Joe Warren
***Hook:*** Daiichi 1710, sizes 14-16
***Thread:*** Color to match body, 6/0
***Body:*** Four or five peacock (tr), root beer (sl), gold (sl), or gunmetal (m) beads, small
***Tail:*** Natural goose biots
***Bead Dressing:*** Clark's Tying Yarn, color to match beads, taper fiber width, short at back, wider at front

**66. Pebble Bead Crayfish**
***Originator:*** Joe Warren
***Hook:*** Daiichi 2320, sizes 2-6
***Thread:*** Brown 6/0
***Tail:*** Red and dark brown Clark's Tying Yarn, half a strand of each, combed together
***Body:*** Five root beer (tr) beads, large
***Bead Dressing:*** Red and dark brown Clark's Tying Yarn, half a strand of each, combed together
***Antennae:*** Red bucktail fibers and two brown hackle stems, stripped
***Claws:*** Brown dyed grizzly hackle notched
***Eyes:*** Red (tr) beads, medium, mounted on 30-pound mono
***Carapace:*** Dark turkey quill
***Legs:*** Brown dyed grizzly hackle
***Thorax:*** Medium brown fur dubbing

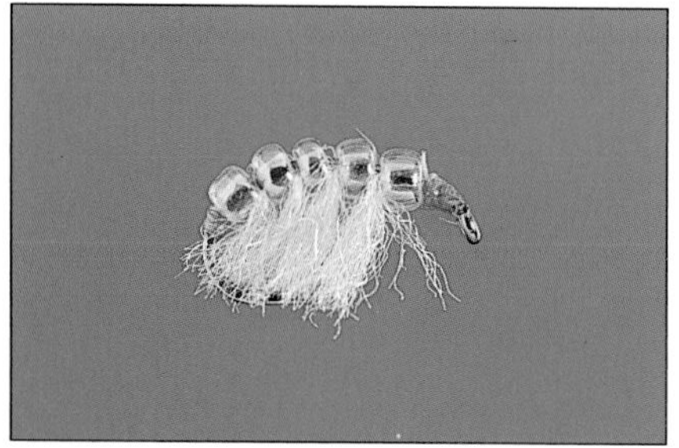

**67. Rainy's Bead Back Scud (dark amber)**
***Originator and Tier:*** Rainy Riding
***Hook:*** Dai-Riki 135, Daiichi 1250, sizes 12-16
***Thread:*** Color to match beads, 8/0
***Body:*** Five or six dark amber (ir) beads, small
***Legs:*** Amber Rainy's Sparkle Dub

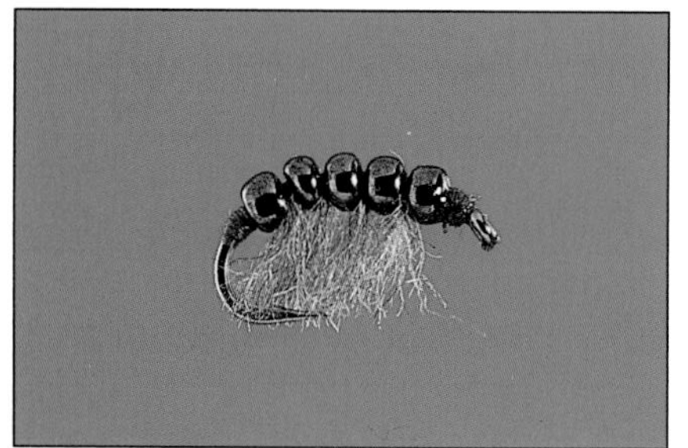

**68. Rainy's Bead Back Scud (olive)**
***Tier:*** Rainy Riding
***Hook:*** Dai-Riki 135, Daiichi 1250, sizes 12-16
***Thread:*** Color to match beads, 8/0
***Body:*** Five or six olive (m) beads, small
***Legs:*** Olive Rainy's Sparkle Dub

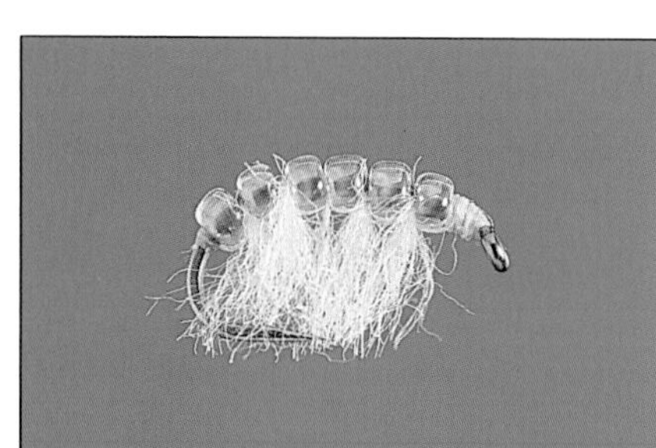

**69. Rainy's Bead Back Scud (shrimp pink)**
***Tier:*** Rainy Riding
***Hook:*** Dai-Riki 135, Daiichi 1250, sizes 12-16
***Thread:*** Color to match beads, 8/0
***Body:*** Five or six shrimp pink (ic, ir) beads, small
***Legs:*** Shrimp pink Rainy's Sparkle Dub

**70. Seed Bead Scud**
***Originator:*** Joe Warren
***Hook:*** Daiichi 1710, sizes 8-14
***Thread:*** Color to match beads, 8/0
***Antennae:*** Partridge, great gadwall, or wood duck flank fibers
***Body:*** Four to six light green, amber, gold, or brown (ir) beads, small
***Tail:*** Partridge, great gadwall, or wood duck flank fibers
***Bead Dressing:*** Hare dubbing, color to match bead, brushed and picked downward for legs

**71. Seed Bead Shrimp**
***Tier:*** Chuck Cameron
***Hook:*** Tiemco 200R, Daiichi 1270, sizes 10-14
***Thread:*** Green or white
***Antennae:*** Yellow dyed grizzly fibers
***Body:*** Four to six neon yellow (ic) beads, small
***Ribbing:*** Fine gold or copper wire
***Tail:*** Same as antennae with fibers from shell back over top
***Bead Dressing:*** Light green fur dubbing
***Shell:*** Deer hair, tips tied in for tail over grizzly hackle fibers

## Worms, Leeches

**72. Bead Banded Earth Worm**
***Hook:*** Daiichi 1510, sizes 14-16
***Thread:*** Red 8/0
***Band:*** Root beer (sl) bead, small
***Body:*** Earthworm Micro Ultra Chenille (1mm)

**73. Glass Hare Worm**
***Hook:*** Mustad 79666, sizes 1/0-6
***Thread:*** Color to suit, 6/0
***Head:*** Scarlet (sl), diamond (sl), peacock (m), or iridescent purple (ir) bead, x-large
***Body:*** Black, purple, chartreuse, white, or burnt orange rabbit strip, one and a half length of hook

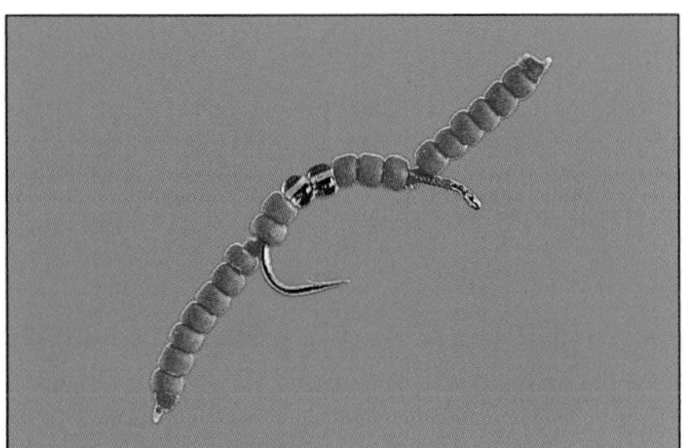

**74. Joe's San Juan Worm**
***Originator:*** Joe Warren
***Hook:*** Daiichi 1130, sizes 10-12
***Thread:*** Red 8/0
***Body:*** Three red frost, two root beer (sl), and two red frost beads, small
***Body (aft and fore):*** Six to eight frosted red beads threaded on red Micro Ultra Chenille (1mm)

**75. Glass Marabou Leech**
***Hook:*** Daiichi 1710, sizes 10-14
***Thread:*** Black or olive 8/0
***Body:*** Five to seven dark blue (sl) or light green (ir) beads, small
***Tail:*** Black or olive marabou tips
***Bead Dressing:*** Several fibers of black or olive marabou fibers

**76. Pebble Sucking Leech**
***Hook:*** Daiichi 1720, sizes 2-10
***Thread:*** Black monocord
***Head:*** Scarlet (sl) bead, x-large or large
***Tail:*** Black marabou tips
***Body:*** Black Steelhead & Salmon Dubbin twisted in dubbing loop with black saddle hackle

## Terrestrials

**77. Joe's Drowning Ant**
***Originator:*** Joe Warren
***Hook:*** Daiichi 1530, sizes 10-12
***Thread:*** Black 6/0
***Body:*** Black bead, medium; two black beads, small; and one black bead, medium
***Butt (optional):*** Scarlet (sl) bead, small
***Legs:*** Black neck hackle

**78. Pebble Bead Woolly Worm**
***Originator:*** Joe Warren
***Hook:*** Daiichi 1280, 1710, sizes 8-10
***Thread:*** Red 8/0
***Body:*** Two red (ir), two black, and two red (ir) beads, medium
***Hackle:*** Grizzly

## Fish Spawn

**79. Golden Egg**
***Originator:*** Joe Warren
***Hook:*** Daiichi 4255, sizes 10-12
***Thread:*** White 6/0
***Body:*** Orange (sl) bead, large
***Tail:*** White marabou tips

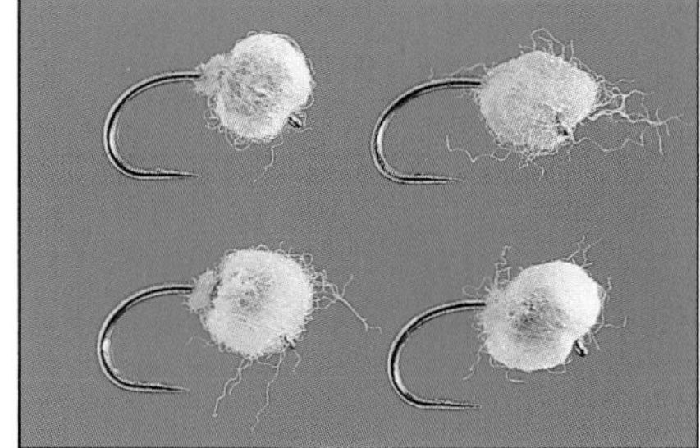

**80. Pettis' Unreal Egg**
***Originator and Tier:*** Jim Pettis
***Hook:*** Tiemco 2457, Daiichi 1510, size 12
***Thread:*** Red 6/0
***Underbody:*** Dark orange (sl) or red (sl) bead, large
***Overbody:*** Peachy king, champagne, apricot, or golden nugget Glo Bug Yarn

**81. Pettis' Unreal Roe**
***Originator and Tier:*** Jim Pettis
***Hook:*** Tiemco 2457, Daiichi 1530, size 10, barbless
***Thread:*** Cream Super Thread
***Underbody:*** Three orange (tr) beads, large
***Overbody:*** Early Girl (light roe), McRoe (dark roe), or pink, McFlyFoam Bug Yarn

# Searching Flies

**Attractor Patterns**
(82-96)

**Streamers and Miscellaneous Baitfish**
(97-111)

Searching flies are fish locaters that provoke an attack. They are the few back-up flies you have stuffed away in your fly box for those occasions when nothing seems to be hatching or scurrying about in the water. Attractor patterns fall under this category and are non-specific imitators that may represent whatever the fish wants it to be: a drowned caddis, a leech, a crayfish, or a minnow.

The flare of color and the brilliant glaze of the glass beads are effective elements for these patterns. Attractor and streamer patterns are often responsible for hooking the largest fish or providing the memory of the big one that broke away.

## Attractor Patterns

**82. 4th of July**
***Originator and Tier:*** Randy Babbitt
***Hook:*** Daiichi 1720, size 10
***Thread:*** Red 6/0
***Body:*** Rear three-fourths alternating three red (tr) and two clear/pearl (sl) beads, small; front fourth metallic blue Lite Brite
***Hackle:*** Dyed red guinea

**83. Glass Carey Special**
***Hook:*** Daiichi 1710, sizes 4-8
***Thread:*** Black 6/0
***Underbody:*** Yellow or light green yarn
***Body:*** Rear three-fourths three olive/pearl (sl) beads, large; front fourth peacock herl
***Tail:*** Pheasant tail fibers
***Hackle:*** Ringneck pheasant blue-gray rump feather

**84. Glass Soft Hackle (black)**
***Originator and Tier:*** Bill Black
***Hook:*** Daiichi 1270, sizes 10-14
***Thread:*** Black 6/0
***Body:*** Five to eight black beads, small
***Thorax:*** Black squirrel or Antron dubbing
***Hackle:*** Black dyed partridge

**85. Glass Soft Hackle (gold)**
***Tier:*** Bill Black
***Hook:*** Daiichi 1270, sizes 10-14
***Thread:*** Yellow 6/0
***Body:*** Five to eight gold/pearl (sl) beads, small
***Thorax:*** Antique gold squirrel or Antron dubbing
***Hackle:*** Brown partridge

**86. Knee Hackle Special**
***Originator and Tier:*** Henry Hoffman
***Hook:*** Mustad 3906B, Daiichi 1560, sizes 10-16
***Thread:*** Brown or dun 8/0
***Head:*** Gold/pearl (sl) bead, medium
***Tail:*** Barred brown or dun Chickabou
***Ribbing:*** Gold wire, counter-wound
***Body:*** Barred brown or dun small Chickabou plumes tied in by tips (body can be tapered by adding underbody)
***Hackle:*** Barred brown or dun Chickabou soft knee hackle

**87. Pebble Bug**
***Hook:*** Daiichi 1750, sizes 2-10
***Thread:*** Black 6/0
***Underbody:*** Black yarn
***Body:*** Four black (m) beads, x-large; and two large black beads
***Tail:*** Gray rubber legs, medium
***Legs:*** Gray rubber legs, medium
***Antennae:*** Gray rubber legs, medium
***Head:*** Black Steelhead & Salmon Dubbin
***Note:*** Use 4 large beads and 2 medium beads on hook sizes 6-10

**88. Pebble Bugger**
***Hook:*** Daiichi 2220, sizes 1-6
***Thread:*** Black 6/0
***Underbody:*** Black yarn
***Body:*** Four to six black (m) beads, x-large
***Tail:*** Purple marabou tips
***Bead Dressing:*** Purple dyed grizzly saddle hackle, tapered
***Attractant:*** One or two strands of pearl Flashabou on each side

**89. Pebble Bugger Diver**
***Hook:*** Daiichi 2220, sizes 1-6
***Thread:*** Olive 6/0
***Head:*** Copper or gold bead (3/16)
***Underbody:*** Dark yarn
***Body:*** Three to five peacock (m) beads, x-large
***Tail:*** Olive marabou tips
***Bead Dressing:*** Olive dyed grizzly saddle hackle, tapered
***Attractant:*** One or two strands of pearl Flashabou on each side

**90. Seed Bead Wet Fly**
***Hook:*** Daiichi 1550, sizes 12-16
***Thread:*** Color to match beads
***Body:*** Three or four beads (ir), small, color to suit
***Tail:*** Soft grizzly hackle fibers
***Hackle:*** Grizzly

**91. Shiny Soft Hackle (blue)**
***Hook:*** Daiichi 1550, sizes 10-14
***Thread:*** Black 8/0
***Thorax:*** Dark blue (sl) bead, small
***Body:*** Black Krystal Flash or floss
***Hackle:*** Light gray partridge

**92. Shiny Soft Hackle (diamond)**
***Hook:*** Daiichi 1550, sizes 10-14
***Thread:*** Olive 8/0
***Thorax:*** Diamond (sl) or crystal (ir) bead, small or medium
***Body:*** Yellow or orange floss
***Hackle:*** Light partridge

**93. Sweet Pea**
***Originator:*** Joe Warren
***Hook:*** Daiichi 1720, sizes 8-12
***Thread:*** Olive 8/0
***Body:*** Six to nine light green (ir) or olive/pearl (sl) beads, small
***Tail:*** Olive marabou fibers pinched off short
***Wing:*** Olive marabou tips to length of tail

**94. Waggle Bugger (black 'n blue)**
***Hook:*** Daiichi 1850, sizes 6-10 for tail; Daiichi 1530, sizes 4-8 for body (body hook one size larger than tail hook)
***Thread:*** Black 6/0
***Underbody (tail):*** Purple or black yarn
***Tail:*** Four to six dark blue (sl) beads, large and black marabou tips (use 12-pound nylon-coated, stainless steel American Fishing Wire to connect tail hook to body)
***Body:*** Black medium chenille
***Hackle:*** Purple dyed grizzly saddle hackle
***Eyes:*** Black nickel Real Eyes (5/32)

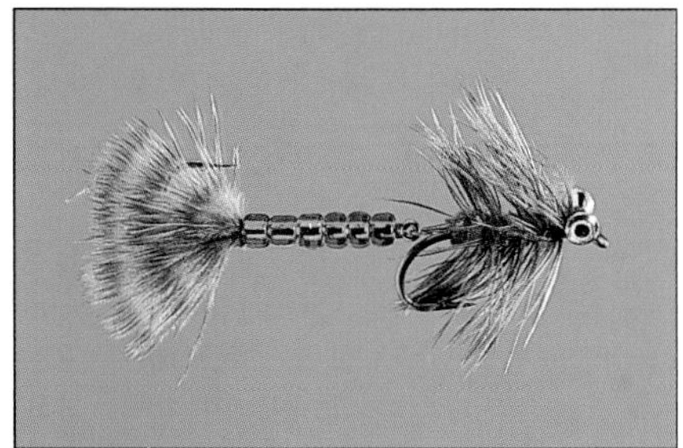

**95. Waggle Bugger (brown)**
***Hook:*** Daiichi 1850, sizes 6-10 for tail; Daiichi 1530, sizes 4-8 for body
***Thread:*** Brown 6/0
***Underbody (tail):*** Brown yarn
***Tail:*** Four to six root beer (sl) beads, large and brown barred Chickabou soft hackle tips (use 12-pound nylon-coated, stainless steel American Fishing Wire to connect tail hook to body)
***Body:*** Brown medium chenille
***Hackle:*** Brown barred Chickabou soft hackle
***Eyes:*** Gold Real Eyes (5/32)

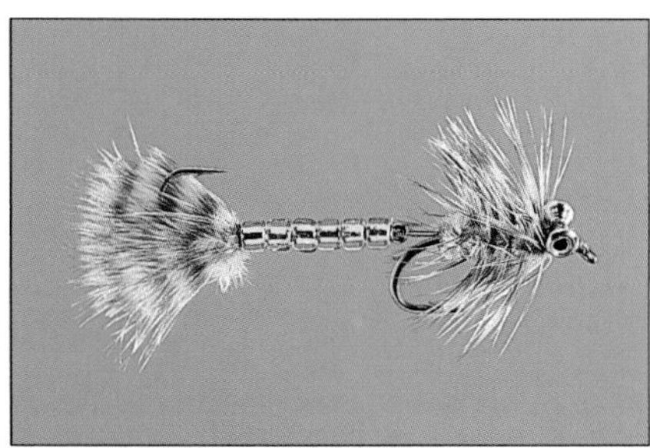

**96. Waggle Bugger (olive)**
***Hook:*** Daiichi 1850, sizes 6-10 for tail; Daiichi 1530, sizes 4-8 for body
***Thread:*** Olive 6/0
***Underbody (tail):*** Olive yarn
***Tail:*** Four to six olive/pearl (sl) beads, large and olive barred Chickabou soft hackle tips (use 12-pound nylon-coated, stainless steel American Fishing Wire to connect tail hook to body)
***Body:*** Olive medium chenille
***Hackle:*** Olive barred Chickabou soft hackle
***Eyes:*** Gold Real Eyes (5/32)

## Streamers & Baitfish

**97. Glass Alevin**
***Hook:*** Daiichi 2220, sizes 8-12
***Thread:*** White or light gray 8/0
***Head:*** Crystal (ir) bead, small and crystal bead, medium
***Body:*** Five to seven crystal (ir) beads, small
***Tail:*** Pearlescent Mylar tubing strands
***Yolk Sac:*** Flame orange Glo Bug Yarn
***Eyes:*** Prismatic eyes coated with epoxy

**98. Glass Chub**
***Hook:*** Daiichi 2220, 2340, sizes 2-6
***Thread:*** Olive 6/0
***Underbody:*** Yellow or green yarn
***Body:*** Six to nine olive/pearl (sl) beads, large
***Tail:*** Four dyed olive grizzly saddle feathers with round tips
***Bead Dressing:*** Dyed olive grizzly saddle hackle fibers, tapered
***Head:*** Dyed olive grizzly saddle hackle fibers, thick
***Cheeks (optional):*** Jungle cock

**99. Glass Ghost**
***Hook:*** Daiichi 2220, sizes 8-12
***Thread:*** Black 8/0
***Body:*** Six black beads alternated with 5 diamond (sl) beads, small
***Tail:*** Yellow marabou tips
***Beard:*** Yellow marabou tips
***Wing:*** White marabou tips

**100. Glass Spruce**
*Hook:* Daiichi 2220, sizes 6-10
*Thread:* Red at tail, black to finish fly, 8/0
*Thorax:* Green/pearl (sl) bead, large and peacock herl
*Body:* Four red (tr) beads, medium
*Tail:* Peacock sword, 4-6 tips
*Wing:* Badger hackle tips, 1-2 pairs
*Hackle:* Badger

**101. Glass 'n Brass Goochie**
*Originator:* Joe Warren
*Hook:* Daiichi 1750, sizes 4-8
*Thread:* Olive 6/0
*Bead Head:* Gold or copper, medium (5/32) or large (3/16)
*Underbody:* Yellow yarn
*Body:* Four to six olive/pearl (sl) beads, large
*Tail:* Olive marabou tips
*Wing:* Chartreuse Lite Brite and olive marabou

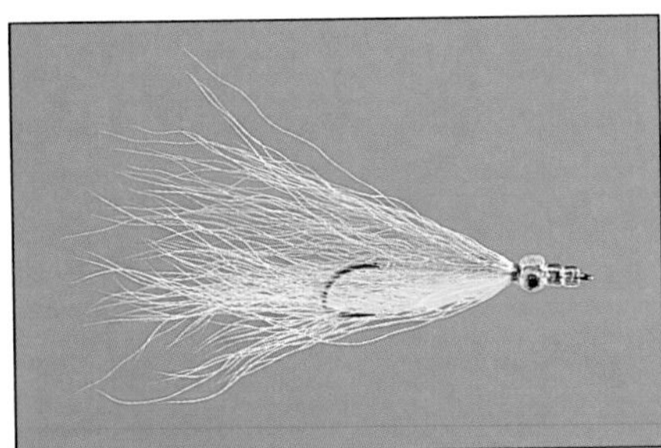

**102. Joe's Bucktail Minnow**
*Originator:* Joe Warren
*Hook:* Daiichi 1750, 2340, 2546, sizes 2-6
*Thread:* White Nymo or monocord
*Snout/Head:* Two diamond (sl) beads, large; one diamond bead, x-large
*Underbody:* White thread
*Body:* Saltwater pearlescent Flashabou
*Belly:* Yellow or white bucktail
*Wing:* Green or gray bucktail
*Eyes:* Small (1/8") adhesive type, coated with clear cement

**103. Joe's Marabou Minnow**
*Originator:* Joe Warren
*Hook:* Daiichi 1750, sizes 2-6
*Thread:* White Nymo or monocord
*Snout/Head:* Two diamond (sl) beads, large; one diamond bead, x-large
*Underbody:* White thread
*Body:* Saltwater pearlescent Flashabou
*Wing:* Marabou, color to suit
*Attractant:* One or two strands of Flashabou, on each side, color to suit

**104. Joe's Sculpin**
*Originator:* Joe Warren
*Hook:* Daiichi 2340, sizes 2-6
*Thread:* Brown 6/0
*Body:* Five to seven tan (tr) beads, large
*Tail:* Four dyed brown grizzly saddle hackle tips
*Bead Dressing:* Dyed brown grizzly saddle hackle, marabou, or rabbit strip fur
*Collar:* Brown marabou
*Pectoral Fins:* Mottled hen neck hackle feathers, 2 per side
*Head:* Light brown deer hair, use black or dark brown waterproof marker for vermiculations
*Eyes:* Red 3-D Hologram eyes, size medium, glued with Marine Goop

**105. Razzma-Tazz Minnow**
*Originator:* Joe Warren
*Hook:* Daiichi 2451, sizes 4-6; Daiichi 2550, sizes 4-6 (for trailer hook)
*Thread:* Tan Kevlar to secure wire on lead hook; Translucent Thread, size fine, to finish
*Body:* Six gold (sl) beads, medium; four gold (sl) beads, large, threaded on 12-pound nylon-coated, stainless steel American Fishing Wire, 3.5" long looped through trailing hook.
*Snout/Head:* Two medium gold (sl) beads; one large gold (sl) bead
*Wing:* Yellow, light green and dark green bucktail
*Throat:* White bucktail
*Eyes:* Red 3-D Hologram, size medium, glued with Marine Goop
*Note:* This pattern is 3 inches in length.

**106. Seed Bead Mickey Finn**
*Hook:* Daiichi 2370, sizes 4-8
*Thread:* Black 6/0
*Body:* Eleven to fifteen white (p) beads, medium
*Wing:* Yellow, red and yellow bucktail

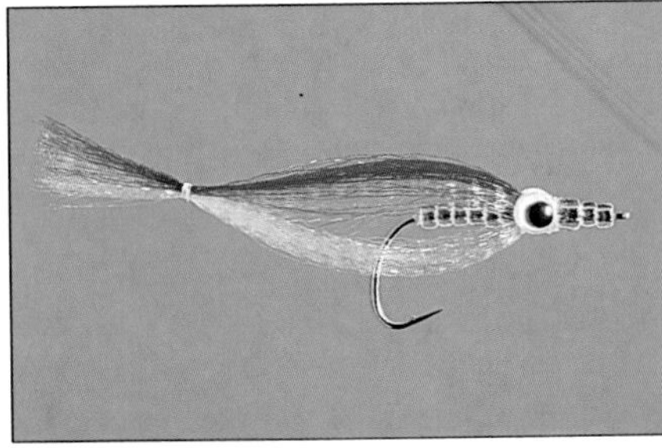

**107. Sultry Shad**
*Originator:* Joe Warren
*Hook:* Daiichi 2722, sizes 3/0-1/0 (for saltwater use Mustad 34011)
*Thread:* Transparent Thread
*Snout/Head:* Two diamond (sl) beads, large; one diamond bead, x-large
*Body:* One diamond bead, x-large; three to five diamond beads, large
*Belly:* White Super Hair
*Topping:* Smoke and blue Super Hair
*Eyes:* White audible eyes, 7mm, glued with Marine Goop
*Tail:* Tie off hair fibers about 3/4 to 1 inch back from end of hair tips and Super Glue
*Note:* This pattern is 3 or 4 inches in length.

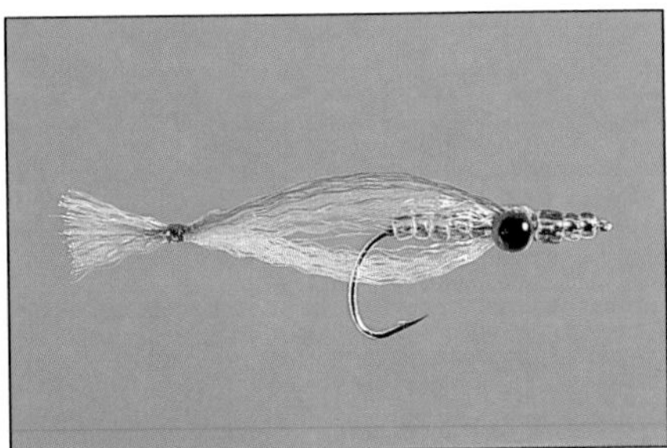

**108. Sultry Shiner**
*Originator:* Joe Warren
*Hook:* Daiichi 2722, sizes 1/0-2
*Thread:* Transparent Thread, fine
*Snout/Head:* Two gold (sl) beads, medium; one gold (sl) bead, large
*Body:* Three to five gold (sl) beads, large
*Belly:* Green/chartreuse Super Hair
*Topping:* Light green and green (sparse) Super Hair
*Eyes:* Red 3-D Hologram, size medium, glue with Marine Goop
*Tail:* Tie off hair fibers about 1/2 to 3/4 inches back from end of hair tips then Super Glue
*Note:* This pattern is 2 to 3 inches in length.

## Long Beaded Streamers

**109. Clark's Glass Bead Streamer**
***Originator and Tier:*** Lee Clark
***Hook:*** Daiichi 2552, size 2, Daiichi 2552, size 6 for trailer hook
***Thread:*** White at trailer hook, black to finish, 6/0
***Body:*** Fifteen to 19 large diamond (sl) beads. Use 30-lb. mono knotted to trailer hook and thread on beads
***Tail:*** Six white saltwater neck hackle tips
***Underbody (front hook):*** Silver tinsel
***OverBody:*** Six white saltwater neck hackle feathers
***Topping:*** Silver and black Krystal Flash
***Cheeks:*** Silver pheasant feather and jungle cock
***Note:*** This pattern is 4 to 5 inches in length.
(***Author's Note:*** Lee Clark's Bead Streamer is my introduction to stringing beads for streamer patterns)

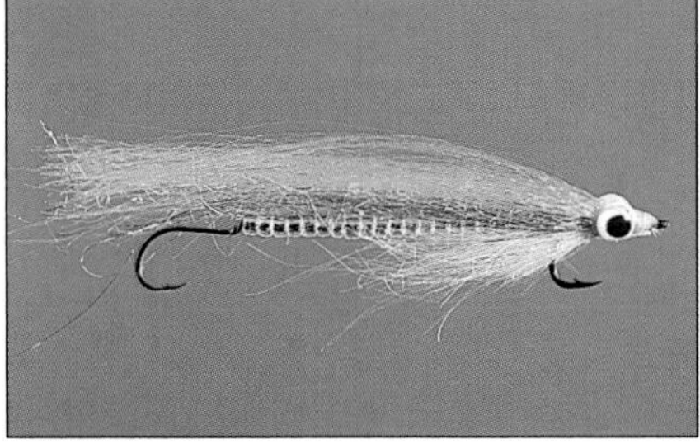

**110. Heat Flash**
***Originator:*** Joe Warren
***Hook:*** Daiichi 2571, size 2, Daiichi 2550, size 2 for trailer hook
***Thread:*** Translucent Thread, fine
***Body:*** Twenty diamond (sl) beads, large, threaded on 18-pound, nylon-coated, stainless steel American Fishing Wire, 7 inches long, looped to trailer hook
***Belly/Throat:*** Polar pearl Lite Brite
***UnderWing:*** Chartreuse Lite Brite
***Wing:*** Green/chartreuse Super Hair and yellow Super Hair
***Eyes:*** White audible eyes, 7mm, glued with Marine Goop
***Note:*** This pattern is 5 inches in length.

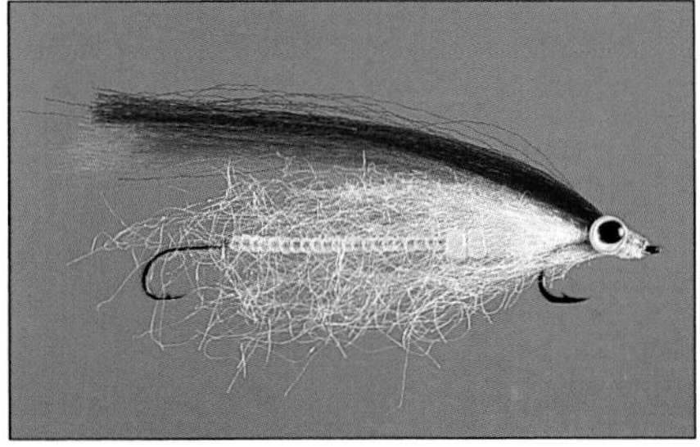

**111. The Streak**
***Originator:*** Joe Warren
***Hook:*** Daiichi 2571, size 2, Daiichi 2550, size 2 for trailer hook
***Thread:*** Translucent Thread, fine
***Body:*** Twenty white (p) beads, medium; four pale pink (p) beads, x- large, threaded on 18-pound, nylon-coated, stainless steel American Fishing Wire, 7 inches long, looped to trailer hook
***Belly/Throat:*** Polar pearl Lite Brite
***Underwing:*** Pearl/blue flash Lite Brite
***Wing:*** Light blue, blue, and dark blue Super Hair
***Eyes:*** White audible eyes, 7mm, glued with Marine Goop
***Note:*** This pattern is 5 inches in length.

# Chapter 8

# Flies for Anadromous Fish

**Steelhead**
(112-151)

**Pacific Salmon**
(154-159)

**Shad**
(160-162)

My first glass-bead fly design was a bead-body fly tied for spring chinook salmon that was successful in hooking these early run fish. Shortly thereafter I began incorporating glass beads into steelhead flies.

The Pacific salmon and steelhead flies were great candidates to experiment with as they are poised with bright and colorful materials. Substituting glass beads for traditional materials produced an attractive fly with positive fishing results. Some steelhead flies have been tied as bead-head flies by using the x-large size bead; in the water they appear to be wearing a headlamp. Interesting effects can be achieved by mixing the bead colors, such as alternating diamond beads with colored beads, or using a bright-colored bead as a butt followed by dark colored beads.

## Steelhead

**112. Bead Boss**
*Tier:* Joe Miltenberger
*Hook:* Alec Jackson Spey, sizes 3-7, blue
*Thread:* Black prewaxed
*Body:* Four scarlet (sl) beads, large
*Tail:* Black wool or marabou
*Hackle:* Black saddle
*Eyes:* Nickel barbell eyes, small or medium

**113. Bead Spider Spruce**
*Tier:* Joe Miltenberger
*Hook:* Alec Jackson Spey, sizes 3-7, bronze
*Thread:* Black prewaxed
*Body:* Three to four green/pearl (sl) beads, large; one yellow or orange (sl) bead, large
*Tail:* Peacock sword, 4-6 tips
*Hackle:* Dyed green mallard, tied sparse

**114. Bead Western Coachman**
*Tier:* Joe Miltenberger
*Hook:* Alec Jackson Spey, sizes 3-7, bronze
*Thread:* Black prewaxed
*Body:* Two to three green/pearl (sl) beads, one scarlet (sl), and one green/pearl (sl) bead, large
*Tail:* Golden pheasant tippets, 5 fibers
*Hackle:* Black saddle
*Collar:* White hackle

**115. Blue Boy**
*Originator:* Joe Warren
*Hook:* Alec Jackson Spey, sizes 3-7, nickel
*Thread:* Black 6/0
*Underbody:* Dark yarn under beads
*Body:* Rear half three dark blue (sl) beads, large; front half black ostrich herl twisted with small oval silver tinsel
*Tail:* Dyed blue guinea feather fibers
*Hackle:* Dyed purple grizzly saddle
*Wing:* Polar bear or white calf tail

**116. Borden Special**
*Tier:* Chuck Cameron
*Hook:* Tiemco 200R, Daiichi 1270, sizes 6-10
*Thread:* Red 8/0
*Body:* Five or six pink (ic) beads, medium
*Bead Dressing:* Pink dubbing, sparse
*Tail:* Yellow and pink hackle fibers
*Wing:* Arctic fox
*Hackle:* Yellow and pink

**117. Brad's Brat**
*Tier:* Chuck Cameron
*Hook:* Tiemco 7999, Daiichi 2161, sizes 4-6
*Thread:* Orange 6/0
*Body:* Three or four scarlet (sl) beads, large; one or two orange (sl) beads, large
*Tail:* White and orange Arctic fox
*Wing:* White and orange Arctic fox
*Hackle:* Brown

**118. Cherry Pie**
*Originator:* Joe Warren
*Hook:* Alec Jackson Spey, sizes 3-7, gold
*Thread:* Red 6/0
*Underbody:* Red yarn under beads
*Body:* Rear half three scarlet (sl) beads, large; front half copper Lite Brite
*Tail:* Golden pheasant crest
*Hackle:* Badger

**119. Columbia Stillwater Orange**
*Originator:* Joe Warren
*Hook:* Bob Veverka's Classic Salmon, size 8, gold
*Thread:* Hot orange 8/0
*Body:* Six orange (p) beads, small
*Tail:* Light and dark orange bucktail fibers, mixed
*Hackle:* Dyed hot orange grizzly palmered dry style
*Eyes:* Orange (sl) beads, small, mounted on 15-pound mono

**120. Crystal Bead Marabou Spey**
*Originator:* Joe Warren
*Hook:* Alec Jackson Spey, sizes 3/0-5, black
*Thread:* Black 6/0
*Body:* Rear three-fourths black floss twisted with small silver tinsel; front fourth crystal (ir) bead, x-large
*Hackle:* Purple marabou
*Collar:* Great gadwall or pintail flank

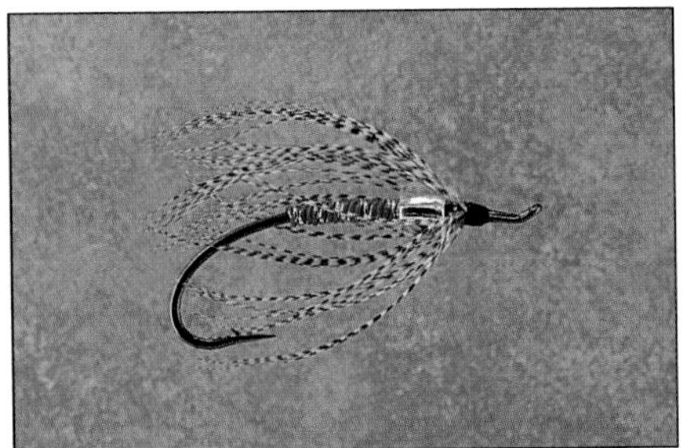

**121. Diamond Soft Serve**
***Originator:*** Joe Warren
***Hook:*** Alec Jackson Spey, sizes 3-5, bronze
***Thread:*** Red 6/0
***Body:*** Rear three-fourths orange floss twisted with small silver tinsel; front fourth x-large diamond (sl) bead
***Hackle:*** Pintail flank

**122. Festival Fly**
***Originator and Tier:*** Joe Miltenberger
***Hook:*** Alec Jackson Spey, sizes 3-5, nickel
***Thread:*** Orange monocord
***Body:*** Four or six orange (sl) beads, large
***Tail:*** Orange and light purple marabou, mixed
***Hackle:*** Orange, yellow, and pink

**123. Fiesta Fly**
***Originator and Tier:*** Joe Miltenberger
***Hook:*** Alec Jackson Spey, sizes 3-5, black
***Thread:*** Red silk prewaxed
***Body:*** Four scarlet (sl) beads, large; one yellow (sl) bead, large
***Tail:*** Red and light purple marabou, mixed
***Hackle:*** Dyed red golden pheasant rump, yellow saddle, and dyed red golden pheasant rump (shorter than first one)

**124. Glass Spawn**
***Originator:*** Joe Warren
***Hook:*** Alec Jackson Spey, sizes 5-7, bronze
***Thread:*** Hot orange 6/0
***Body:*** Two ruby red (sl) beads, x-large
***Tail:*** Orange hackle fibers
***Hackle:*** White

**125. Glassy Marabou (Ace of Spades)**
***Originator and Tier:*** Randy Babbitt
***Hook:*** Alec Jackson Spey, size 3, gold
***Thread:*** Black 3/0
***Underbody (optional):*** Lead wire, .010"
***Body:*** Three black (m) beads, x-large
***Tag:*** Holographic Fly Flash
***Underwing:*** Gray squirrel
***Wing:*** Black marabou
***Hackle:*** Natural guinea

**126. Glassy Marabou (Crystal Blue Persuasion)**
***Tier:*** Randy Babbitt
***Hook:*** Alec Jackson Spey, size 3, gold
***Thread:*** Black 3/0
***Underbody:*** Holographic Fly Flash
***Body:*** Three iridescent blue (ir) beads, x-large
***Tail:*** Silver dun marabou
***Butt:*** Holographic Fly Flash
***Wing:*** Silver dun and peacock blue marabou, mixed
***Hackle:*** Dyed blue guinea

**127. Glassy Marabou (Irish Gold)**
***Tier:*** Randy Babbitt
***Hook:*** Alec Jackson Spey, size 3, gold
***Thread:*** Black 3/0
***Body:*** Three bottle green (sl) beads, x-large
***Tail:*** Insect green marabou
***Butt:*** Holographic Fly Flash
***Wing:*** Insect green and yellow marabou, mixed
***Hackle:*** Dyed yellow and green guinea

**128. Glassy Marabou (Leprechaun)**
***Tier:*** Randy Babbitt
***Hook:*** Alec Jackson Spey, size 3, gold
***Thread:*** Black 3/0
***Body:*** Rear three-fourths three peacock (m) beads, x-large; front fourth green Lite Brite
***Tail:*** Black marabou
***Butt:*** Holographic Fly Flash
***Wing:*** Black marabou
***Hackle:*** Dyed right green guinea

**129. Glassy Marabou (Mary's Purple Charm)**
***Tier:*** Randy Babbitt
***Hook:*** Alec Jackson Spey, size 3, gold
***Thread:*** Black 3/0
***Underbody:*** Holographic Fly Flash
***Body:*** Three iridescent purple (ir) beads, x-large
***Tail:*** Black and purple marabou, mixed
***Butt:*** Holographic Fly Flash
***Wing:*** Purple, black and white marabou, mixed
***Hackle:*** Natural guinea

**130. Glassy Marabou (Pink Panther)**
***Originator and Tier:*** Marrisa Babbitt (age 12)
***Hook:*** Alec Jackson Spey, size 3, gold
***Thread:*** Black 3/0
***Body:*** Three pale pink beads, x-large
***Tail:*** Pink marabou with dyed hot pink guinea, sparse
***Butt:*** Holographic Fly Flash
***Wing:*** Pink and white marabou, mixed
***Hackle:*** Dyed hot pink guinea

**131. Glassy Marabou (Sweeter Than Wine)**
***Tier:*** Randy Babbitt
***Hook:*** Alec Jackson Spey, size 3, gold
***Thread:*** Black 3/0
***Underbody:*** Holographic Fly Flash
***Body:*** Three iridescent purple (ir) beads, x-large
***Tail:*** Maroon marabou
***Butt:*** Holographic Fly Flash
***Wing:*** Maroon and white marabou, mixed
***Hackle:*** Natural guinea

**132. Glassy Marabou (Tequila Slammer)**
***Tier:*** Randy Babbitt
***Hook:*** Alec Jackson Spey, size 3, gold
***Thread:*** Black 3/0
***Underbody:*** Holographic Fly Flash
***Body:*** Three crystal (ir) beads, x-large
***Tail:*** Red and yellow marabou, mixed
***Butt:*** Holographic Fly Flash
***Wing:*** Red and yellow marabou, mixed
***Hackle:*** Dyed orange guinea

**133. Hi Beam**
***Originator:*** Joe Warren
***Hook:*** Alec Jackson Spey, sizes 3-5, nickel
***Thread:*** Red 6/0
***Underbody:*** Yellow yarn under beads
***Body:*** Rear half three yellow (sl) beads, large; front half peacock herl twisted with small silver tinsel
***Tail:*** Peacock sword, 4-6 fibers
***Hackle:*** Grizzly

**134. Joe's October Caddis**
***Originator:*** Joe Warren
***Hook:*** Alec Jackson Spey, size 7, bronze
***Thread:*** Dark orange 6/0
***Underbody:*** Orange yarn
***Body:*** Five orange (sl) beads, large
***Butt:*** Black hare dubbing
***Hackle:*** Brown partridge
***Head:*** Black ostrich herl

**135. Neon Nymph**
***Originator:*** Joe Warren
***Hook:*** Alec Jackson Spey, sizes 3-7, nickel
***Thread:*** Orange 6/0
***Underbody:*** Orange yarn
***Body:*** Four or five orange (sl) beads, large
***Tail:*** White goose biots
***Antennae:*** Same as tail
***Thorax:*** Base wrap with .025" or .030" lead (optional), yellow ostrich herl palmer over with dyed hot orange grizzly saddle hackle

**136. Pebble Bead Green Butt Skunk**
***Hook:*** Alec Jackson Spey, sizes 3-5, blue
***Thread:*** Black 6/0
***Underbody:*** black yarn under black beads
***Body:*** Four black beads and one yellow (sl) bead, large
***Tail:*** Red hackle fibers
***Hackle:*** Black
***Wing:*** Polar bear or white calf tail

**137. Pebble Bead Purple Peril**
***Hook:*** Alec Jackson Spey, sizes 3-5, blue
***Thread:*** Gray 6/0
***Underbody:*** Purple yarn
***Body:*** Alternating three dark blue(sl) and two light blue (sl) beads, large
***Tag:*** Flat silver tinsel
***Tail:*** Purple hackle tips
***Hackle:*** Purple
***Wing:*** Dyed purple fox squirrel

**138. Pebble Bead Silver Hilton**
***Hook:*** Alec Jackson Spey, sizes 3-5, black
***Thread:*** Black 6/0
***Underbody:*** Black yarn
***Body:*** Alternating three black and two diamond (sl) beads, large
***Tail:*** Great gadwall flank fibers
***Wing:*** One pair of grizzly hackle tips, flared
***Hackle:*** Grizzly

**139. Pebble Bead Skykomish Sunrise**
***Hook:*** Alec Jackson Spey, sizes 3-5, bronze
***Thread:*** Red 6/0
***Underbody:*** Red yarn
***Body:*** Alternating three scarlet (sl) and two diamond (sl) beads, large
***Tag:*** Flat silver tinsel
***Tail:*** Yellow and red hackle fibers, mixed
***Hackle:*** Yellow and red
***Wing:*** Polar bear or white calf tail

**140. Pebble Bead Steelhead Scud**
***Originator:*** Joe Warren
***Tier:*** Dennis Brown
***Hook:*** Daiichi 2571, sizes 6-8
***Thread:*** Orange 8/0
***Body:*** Four amber (sl) beads, large
***Tail:*** Two hot orange rubber legs
***Bead Dressing:*** Hot orange Steelhead & Salmon Dubbin

**141. Pebble Bead Stillaguamish Sunrise**
***Hook:*** Alec Jackson Spey, sizes 3-5, bronze
***Thread:*** Red 6/0
***Underbody:*** Yellow yarn
***Body:*** Alternating three yellow (sl) and two diamond (sl) beads, large
***Tail:*** Dyed red and yellow guinea fibers
***Hackle:*** Orange
***Wing:*** Polar bear or white calf tail

**142. Pebble Bead Thor**
***Hook:*** Alec Jackson Spey, sizes 3-5, bronze
***Thread:*** Red 6/0
***Underbody:*** Red yarn
***Body:*** Four or five scarlet (sl) beads, large
***Tail:*** Orange hackle tips
***Hackle:*** Brown
***Wing:*** Polar bear or white calf tail

**143. Ravishing Ruby**
***Originator:*** Joe Warren
***Hook:*** Alec Jackson Spey, sizes 1 1/2-5, blue
***Thread:*** 6/0; white for tip, black for body and hackle, hot red to finish
***Head:*** Ruby red (sl) bead, x-large
***Tag:*** Flat silver tinsel
***Tip:*** Hot pink floss
***Tail:*** Golden pheasant crest
***Ribbing:*** Fine oval silver tinsel
***Body:*** Black yarn
***Hackle:*** Black

**144. Royal Rogan**
***Tier:*** Randy Mock
***Hook:*** Daiichi 2161, sizes 1-4
***Thread:*** Chartreuse 6/0
***Body:*** Rear half chartreuse floss; front half three to four dark blue (m), large
***Tag:*** Flat gold tinsel
***Wing:*** Deep purple marabou tied in between beads; black marabou at front (optional)
***Hackle:*** Peacock breast feather

**145. Ruby & Pearls**
***Originator:*** Joe Warren
***Hook:*** Alec Jackson Spey, size 5-7, bronze
***Thread:*** White 6/0
***Head:*** One ruby red (sl) bead, x-large
***Body:*** Five or six pearl (ir) beads, medium
***Tail:*** Hot pink marabou

**146. Sauk River Glass Shrimp (diamond)**
***Hook:*** Alec Jackson Spey, sizes 1/2-3, nickel
***Thread:*** Gray 6/0
***Underbody:*** Gray or white yarn
***Body:*** Four diamond (sl) beads, x-large
***Tail:*** Blue bucktail
***Bead Dressing:*** Light purple saddle hackle tapered, two wraps between each bead
***Hackle:*** Kingfisher blue
***Collar:*** Dyed blue guinea

**147. Sauk River Glass Shrimp (dark)**
***Hook:*** Alec Jackson Spey, sizes 3/0-3, black
***Thread:*** Black 6/0
***Underbody:*** Black yarn
***Body:*** Four black (m) beads, x-large
***Tail:*** Purple bucktail
***Bead Dressing:*** Dyed purple grizzly saddle hackle tapered, two wraps between each bead
***Hackle:*** Dyed purple grizzly
***Collar:*** Dyed red guinea

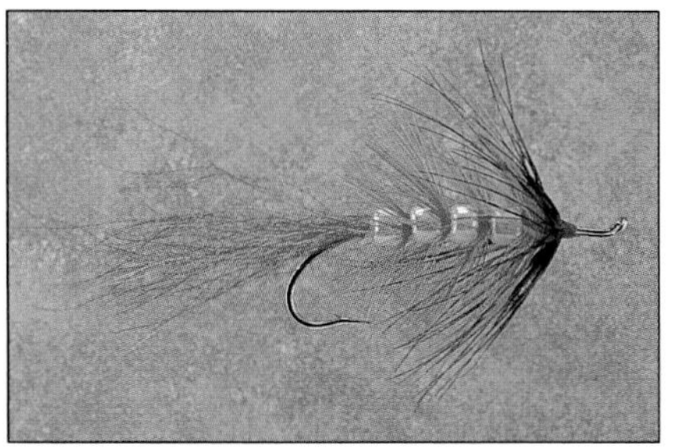

**148. Sauk River Glass Shrimp (pink)**
***Hook:*** Alec Jackson Spey, sizes 1 1/2-3, nickel
***Thread:*** Hot orange 6/0
***Underbody:*** Pink yarn
***Body:*** Four pale pink beads, x-large
***Tail:*** Pink bucktail
***Bead Dressing:*** Pink saddle hackle tapered, two wraps between each bead
***Hackle:*** Pink
***Collar:*** Dyed red guinea

**149. Sauk River Glass Shrimp (red/yellow)**
***Hook:*** Alec Jackson Spey, sizes 3/0-3, gold
***Thread:*** Red 6/0
***Underbody:*** Red yarn
***Body:*** Four ruby red (sl) beads, x-large
***Tail:*** Orange bucktail
***Bead Dressing:*** Yellow saddle hackle tapered, two wraps between each bead
***Hackle:*** Yellow
***Collar:*** Dyed yellow guinea
***Note:*** This pattern is highly recommended for spring chinook salmon, omit collar.

**150. Seed Bead Glo Bug**
***Originator:*** Joe Warren
***Hook:*** Daiichi 1270, sizes 6-10
***Thread:*** White at rear and tan Kevlar to tie Glo Bug
***Body:*** Four or six pink (ic) beads, medium
***Tail:*** White or pink marabou
***Egg:*** Champagne and flame orange (for eye) Glo Bug Yarn

**151. Silver & Gold**
***Originator:*** Joe Warren
***Hook:*** Alec Jackson Spey, sizes 1 1/2-5, gold
***Thread:*** Hot orange 6/0
***Head:*** Diamond (sl) bead, x-large
***Tail:*** Two stems of golden pheasant tippets, dull sides faced in
***Ribbing:*** Small gold wire
***Body:*** Flat gold tinsel
***Hackle:*** Yellow and orange

**152. Steelhead Stone**
***Originator:*** Joe Warren
***Hook:*** Alec Jackson Spey, sizes 3-7, bronze
***Thread:*** Brown 6/0
***Underbody:*** Brown yarn
***Body:*** Four or five root beer (sl) beads, large
***Tail:*** Brown goose biots
***Antennae:*** Same as tail
***Thorax:*** Base wrap with .025" or .030" lead (optional), brown ostrich herl palmer over with grizzly saddle hackle

**153. Sweet Sapphire**
***Originator:*** Joe Warren
***Hook:*** Alec Jackson Spey, sizes 1 1/2-5, nickel
***Thread:*** Gray 6/0
***Head:*** Iridescent blue (ir) bead, x-large
***Tail:*** Purple and kingfisher blue hackle fibers, mixed
***Ribbing:*** Fine silver wire
***Body:*** Flat silver tinsel
***Hackle:*** Purple and kingfisher blue, a couple wraps each
***Collar:*** Natural guinea

## Pacific Salmon

**154. Glass Comet (hot yellow)**
***Hook:*** Alec Jackson Spey, sizes 3-5, gold
***Thread:*** Yellow or chartreuse, 6/0
***Underbody:*** Yellow yarn
***Body:*** Four or five yellow (sl) beads, large
***Tail:*** Insect green bucktail
***Hackle:*** Chartreuse
***Eyes:*** Large silver chain bead

**155. Glass Comet (orange)**
***Hook:*** Alec Jackson Spey, sizes 3-5, nickel
***Thread:*** Orange 6/0
***Underbody:*** Orange yarn
***Body:*** Four or five orange (sl) beads, large
***Tail:*** Orange bucktail
***Hackle:*** Orange
***Eyes:*** Large silver chain bead

**156. King's Sorceress (bright orange)**
***Originator:*** Joe Warren
***Hook:*** Daiichi 2451, sizes 4-6; Daiichi 2550, size 6 for trailer hook (optional)
***Thread:*** Hot orange 6/0, tan Kevlar to secure wire on hook
***Body:*** Three orange (sl) beads, large
***Tail:*** Nine to twelve orange (sl) beads, small, threaded on 12-pound, nylon-coated, stainless steel American Fishing Wire with an A1 crimp sleeve. Cut sleeve in half after crimping into place and tie on rainbow Krystal Flash
***Hackle:*** Dyed hot orange grizzly
***Eyes:*** Diamond (sl) beads, medium, mounted on 30-pound mono

**157. King's Sorceress (hot yellow)**
***Originator:*** Joe Warren
***Hook:*** Daiichi 2451, sizes 4-6; Daiichi 2550, size 6 for trailer hook (optional)
***Thread:*** Chartreuse 6/0, tan Kevlar to secure wire on hook
***Body:*** Three yellow (sl) beads, large
***Tail:*** Nine to twelve yellow (sl) beads, small, threaded on 12-pound, nylon-coated, stainless steel American Fishing Wire 3 inches long, looped through trailer hook with rainbow Krystal Flash
***Hackle:*** Dyed chartreuse grizzly
***Eyes:*** Yellow (tr) beads, medium mounted on 30-pound mono

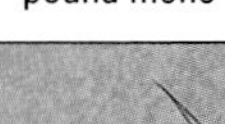

**158. Pink Mistress**
***Originator:*** Joe Warren
***Hook:*** Daiichi 2220, sizes 6-8
***Thread:*** Red 6/0
***Body:*** Six pink (ic) beads, medium
***Tail:*** Black marabou with red Krystal Flash on top 2/3 of marabou length
***Bead Dressing:*** Light brown hackle palmered one or two wraps between the beads
***Eyes:*** Small silver chain bead

**159. Spring Favorite**
***Hook:*** Alec Jackson Spey, size 1 1/2, nickel
***Thread:*** White monocord
***Body:*** Five diamond (sl) beads, x-large
***Tail:*** Orange marabou
***Hackle:*** Orange
***Wing:*** Polar pearl Lite Brite
***Eyes:*** Large silver chain bead

## Shad

**160. Diamond Shad**
***Hook:*** Alec Jackson Spey, size 7, nickel
***Thread:*** White 8/0
***Body:*** One scarlet (sl) bead, large; four diamond (sl) beads, medium
***Tail:*** White marabou and pearl Krystal Flash, mixed
***Hackle:*** White
***Eyes:*** Small silver chain bead

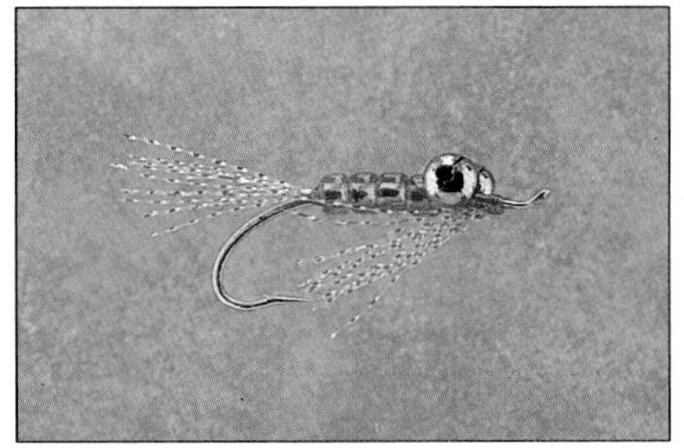

**161. Marigold Shad**
***Hook:*** Alec Jackson Spey, size 7, gold
***Thread:*** Orange 6/0
***Body:*** Four orange (sl) beads, large
***Tail:*** Pearl Krystal Flash
***Eyes:*** Large silver chain bead
***Beard:*** Pearl Krystal Flash

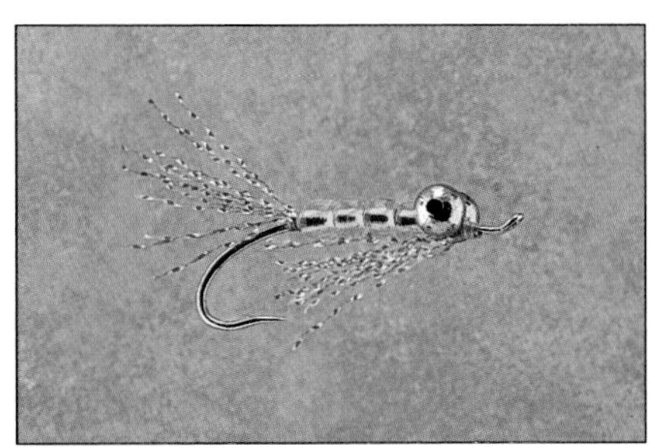

**162. Sunshine Shad**
***Hook:*** Alec Jackson Spey, size 7, nickel
***Thread:*** Yellow 6/0
***Body:*** Four yellow (sl) beads, large
***Tail:*** Rainbow Krystal Flash
***Eyes:*** Large silver chain bead
***Beard:*** Rainbow Krystal Flash

*Chapter 9*

# Saltwater Flies

**Saltwater**
(163-182)

Fly fishing in saltwater is the true test for bead flies. Very few species are more tenacious or aggressive when taking flies than the marine fishes. After thorough field testing, glass beads have survived brutal assaults from at least 20 different saltwater species from Baja to the Oregon Coast. From this, I am convinced of their durability and am pleased that glass beads are indeed well suited for any type of fly and have a vast range of uses in fly fishing.

As previously illustrated, shiny and translucent glass beads continue to work well for imitating saltwater prey, such as shrimp or baitfish, just as they do for fresh-water imitations.

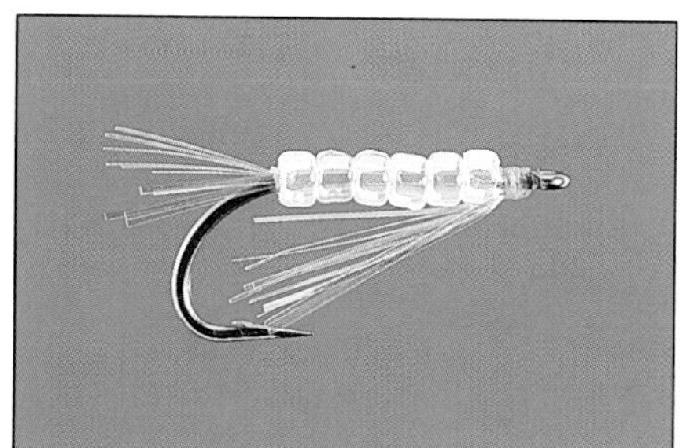

**163. Glassabou Euphausid**
***Hook:*** Daiichi 2546, sizes 4-6
***Thread:*** White 6/0
***Body:*** Six white (ir) beads, medium
***Tail:*** Pearl Flashabou
***Throat:*** Pearl Flashabou

**164. Glass 'N Brass Surf Crab**
***Hook:*** Daiichi 2546, sizes 2-6
***Thread:*** Olive 6/0
***Bead Head:*** Brass bead, medium (5/32) or large (3/16)
***Body:*** Four olive/pearl (sl) beads, large
***Tail/Shellback:*** Dark olive Lite Brite
***Legs:*** Hot orange grizzly hackle wrapped between beads

**165. Glass Surf Percher**
***Hook:*** Daiichi 2546, sizes 2-6
***Thread:*** Hot red or red 6/0
***Body:*** Four gold (sl) beads, large
***Tail:*** Fluorescent yellow marabou
***Wing:*** Fluorescent flame red marabou tips tied between beads; at head tie in orange Krystal Flash, marabou, and red Flashabou
***Eyes:*** Small nickel barbell eyes

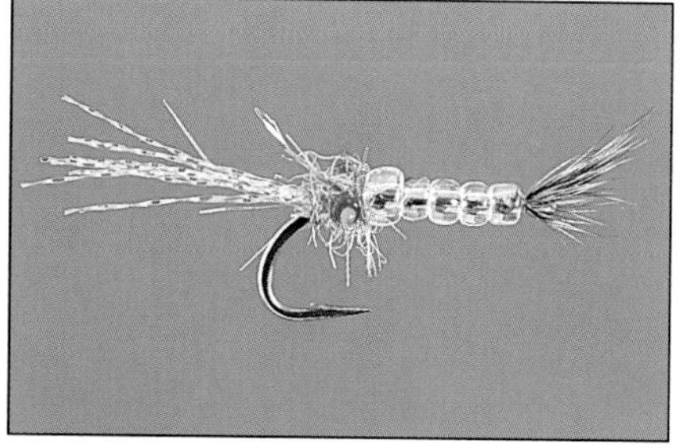

**166. Glow Shrimp (crystal)**
***Originator:*** Joe Warren
***Hook:*** Daiichi 2546, size 6
***Thread:*** White 6/0
***Tail:*** Grizzly hackle fibers
***Body:*** Four crystal (ir) beads, medium; one crystal (ir) bead, large
***Antennae:*** Pearl Krystal Flash
***Eyes:*** Scarlet (sl) beads, small, mounted on 15-pound mono
***Head:*** Hot pink Lite Brite

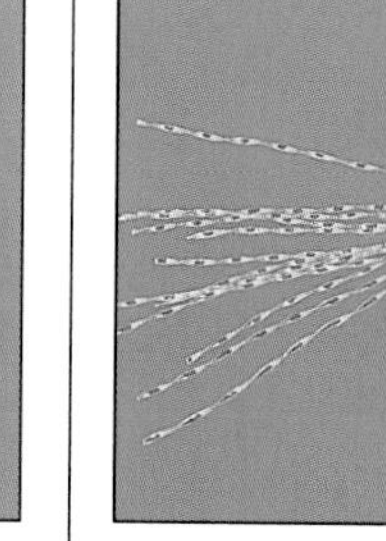

**167. Glow Shrimp (gold)**
***Originator:*** Joe Warren
***Hook:*** Daiichi 2546, size 6
***Thread:*** Yellow 6/0
***Tail:*** Dyed brown grizzly
***Body:*** Four gold (sl) beads, medium; one gold (sl) bead, large
***Antennae:*** Root beer Krystal Flash
***Eyes:*** Scarlet (sl) beads, small, mounted on 15-pound mono
***Head:*** Gold Lite Brite

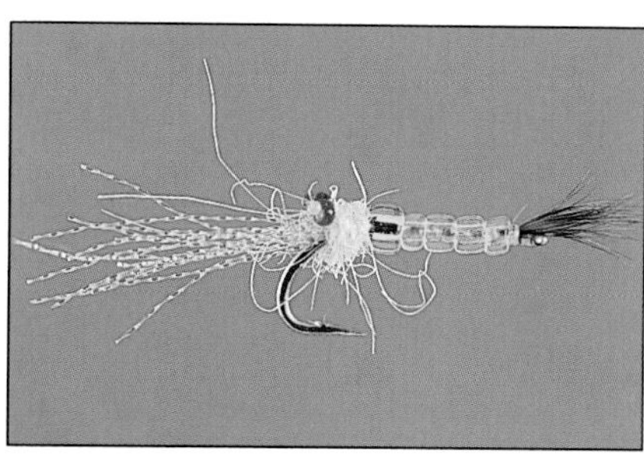

**168. Glow Shrimp (yellow)**
***Hook:*** Daiichi 2546, size 6
***Thread:*** Yellow 6/0
***Tail:*** Dyed hot orange grizzly hackle fibers
***Body:*** Four yellow (tr) beads, medium; one yellow (sl) bead, large
***Antennae:*** Orange Krystal Flash
***Eyes:*** Scarlet (sl) beads, small, mounted on 15-pound mono
***Head:*** Hot yellow Lite Brite

**169. Seed Bead Charlie (light gold)**
***Hook:*** Daiichi 2546, sizes 4-6
***Thread:*** White 6/0
***Body:*** Four or five pale yellow (ic) beads, medium
***Tail:*** Root beer Krystal Flash
***Eyes:*** Small silver chain bead
***Wing:*** Yellow Lite Brite

**170. Seed Bead Charlie (pink & pearl)**
***Hook:*** Daiichi 2546, sizes 4-6
***Thread:*** White 8/0
***Body:*** Four or five pink (ic) beads, medium
***Tail:*** Pearl Krystal Flash
***Eyes:*** Small silver chain bead
***Wing:*** Polar pearl Lite Brite

**171. Seed Bead Charlie (yellow)**
***Hook:*** Daiichi 2546, sizes 4-6
***Thread:*** Yellow 8/0
***Body:*** Five yellow (tr) beads, medium
***Tail:*** Yellow Krystal Flash
***Eyes:*** Small silver chain bead
***Wing:*** Hot yellow Lite Brite

**172. Sparkle Surf Bug (pink & pearl)**
***Hook:*** Daiichi 2546, sizes 2-6
***Thread:*** White 6/0
***Bead Head:*** Brass bead, medium (5/32)
***Body:*** Four crystal (ir) beads, large
***Tail:*** Hot pink marabou
***Bead Dressing:*** Pearl hot pink Estaz

**173. Sparkle Surf Bug (red)**
***Hook:*** Daiichi 2546, sizes 2-6
***Thread:*** Red 6/0
***Bead Head:*** Brass bead, medium (5/32)
***Body:*** Four scarlet (sl) beads, large
***Tail:*** Red marabou
***Bead Dressing:*** Peach Estaz

**174. Sparkle Surf Bug (yellow)**
***Hook:*** Daiichi 2546, sizes 2-6
***Thread:*** Yellow 6/0
***Bead Head:*** Brass bead, medium (5/32)
***Body:*** Four yellow (sl) beads, large
***Tail:*** Yellow marabou
***Bead Dressing:*** Deep red Estaz

**175. The Assassin (blue)**
***Originator:*** Joe Warren
***Hook:*** Daiichi 2546, standard saltwater hook, size 3/0-1/0
***Thread:*** Kevlar, tan
***Tail:*** Light blue pearlescent saltwater Flashabou inserted into wire loop with crimping sleeve drawn tight
***Body:*** Twelve light blue (sl) beads, large; six iridescent blue (ir) beads, x-large, threaded on 40-pound, nylon-coated, stainless steel American Fishing Wire, 7 inches long and looped in half through a #3 crimping sleeve
***Snout/Head:*** Two peacock (m) beads, x-large
***Belly:*** Smoke Super Hair
***Wing:*** Blue bucktail
***Topping:*** Dark blue Super Hair
***Throat:*** White bucktail
***Gills:*** Hot red bucktail
***Eyes:*** White audible eyes, 7mm, glued with Marine Goop
***Note:*** This pattern is 4 to 6 inches in length.

**176. The Assassin, herring**
***Hook:*** Daiichi 2546, standard saltwater hook, size 3/0-1/0
***Thread:*** Kevlar, tan
***Tail:*** Light blue pearlescent saltwater Flashabou inserted into wire loop with crimping sleeve drawn tight
***Body:*** Twelve diamond (sl) beads, large; six diamond (sl) beads, x-large threaded on 40-pound, nylon-coated, stainless steel American Fishing Wire, 7 inches long and looped in half through a #3 crimping sleeve
***Snout/Head:*** Two diamond (sl) beads, x-large on 3/0 hook, otherwise use two large beads and one x-large bead for smaller hooks
***Wing:*** Blue bucktail
***Topping:*** Dark green Super Hair
***Throat:*** White bucktail
***Gills:*** Hot red bucktail
***Eyes:*** White audible eyes, 7mm, glued with Marine Goop
***Note:*** This pattern is 4 to 6 inches in length.

**177. The Assassin (yellow and green)**
***Hook:*** Daiichi 2546, standard saltwater hook, size 3/0-1/0
***Thread:*** Kevlar, tan
***Tail:*** Light green pearlescent saltwater Flashabou
***Body:*** Twelve to fifteen yellow (sl) beads, large; three or four bottle green (sl) beads, x-large threaded on 40-pound, nylon-coated, stainless steel American Fishing Wire, 7 inches long and looped in half through an A3 crimping sleeve
***Snout/Head:*** Two diamond (sl) beads, x-large
***Belly:*** White bucktail
***Wing:*** Light green bucktail
***Topping:*** Peacock herl, 10-12 fibers
***Cheeks:*** Dark bucktail fibers from dyed green tail
***Eyes:*** White audible eyes, 7mm, glued with Marine Goop
***Note:*** This pattern is 4 to 6 inches in length.

**178. Black and Orange with Glass**
***Hook:*** Daiichi 2546, sizes 2/0-1/0
***Thread:*** Color to match beads, 6/0
***Body:*** Four gunmetal (m) beads, large; one gunmetal (m) bead, x-large
***Tail:*** Four orange saddle hackle tips enclosed by four black saddle hackle tips, flared
***Hackle:*** Black and orange, mixed

**179. Glass Squid**
***Originator:*** Joe Warren
***Hook:*** Eagle Claw 66SS, Mustad 34011, 79573, sizes 3/0-1
***Thread:*** White monocord
***Body:*** Four creamy white (ir) beads, x-large
***Tail:*** Six to eight white saddle hackles (include fluff at base) with a strand of pearl saltwater Flashabou on each side. Use white chenille to construct foundation where eyes are glued into place
***Eyes:*** White audible eyes, 7mm, glued with Marine Goop
***Bead Dressing:*** White saddle hackle, two wraps between each bead
***Note:*** This pattern is 4 to 5 inches in length.

**180. Jaw Breaker**
***Originator and Tier:*** Dennis Brown
***Hook:*** Mustad 34011, sizes 2/0-1/0
***Thread:*** Silver 3/0
***Underbody:*** Copenhagen blue floss
***Body:*** Four or five pearl (ir) Killer Caddis beads, x-large
***Tail:*** White marabou
***Lateral Line:*** Peacock herl
***Underwing:*** Layered Krystal Flash, chartreuse and royal blue
***Back:*** Grizzly rabbit fur strip
***Eyes:*** Temple Fork Lazer Eyes
***Head Finish:*** Hot Glue

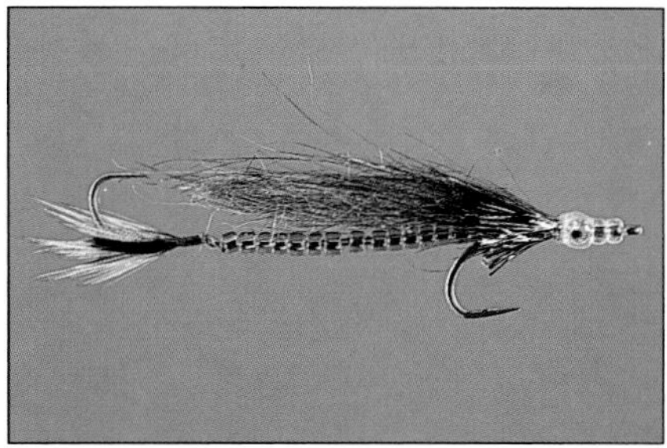

**181. Joe's Sand Lance (aquamarine)**
***Originator:*** Joe Warren
***Hook:*** Daiichi 2546, sizes 2-4, Daiichi 2556, sizes 4-6 for trailer hook (use one size smaller than for ward hook)
***Thread:*** Olive 6/0 for tail, Kevlar to secure wire on front hook, and fine Translucent Thread to finish
***Tail:*** On trailer hook four to six badger hackle tips, notch out tip of feather to form forked tail
***Body:*** Fifteen light blue (sl) beads, large, threaded on 18-pound, nylon-coated, stainless steel American Fishing Wire, 7 inches long and looped in half through trailer hook
***Snout/Head:*** Two crystal (ir) beads, large; one crystal (ir) bead, x-large
***Wing:*** River green Lite Brite
***Topping:*** Dark olive Lite Brite
***Cheeks:*** Silver Flashabou
***Eyes:*** Lazer Eyes, small
***Note:*** This pattern is 3 or 4 inches in length.

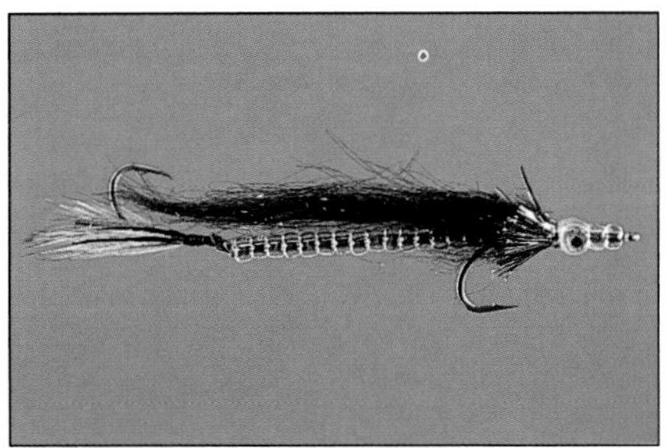

**182. Joe's Sand Lance (diamond)**
***Hook:*** Daiichi 2546, sizes 2-4, Daiichi 2556, sizes 4-6 for trailer (use one size smaller than forward hook)
***Thread:*** Olive 6/0 for tail, Kevlar to secure wire on front hook, and fine Translucent Thread to finish
***Tail:*** On trailer hook four to six badger hackle tips, notch out tip of feather to form forked tail
***Body:*** Fifteen diamond (sl) beads, large, threaded on 18-pound, nylon-coated, stainless steel American Fishing Wire, 7 inches long looped in half through trailer hook
***Snout/Head:*** Two crystal (ir) beads, large; one crystal (ir) bead, x-large
***Wing:*** Dark olive Lite Brite
***Cheeks:*** Silver Flashabou
***Eyes:*** Lazer Eyes, small
***Note:*** This pattern is 3 or 4 inches in length.

# Bibliography

Bates, Jr., Joseph D., *Streamer Fly Fishing In Fresh and Salt Water.* New York: D. Van Nostram Company, Inc., 1950.

Ferguson, Bruce, Les Johnson, and Pat Trotter, *Fly Fishing for Pacific Salmon.* Portland, Oregon: Frank Amato Publications, Inc. 1985.

Hart, J.L., *Pacific Fishes of Canada.* Ottawa, Canada: Fisheries Research Board of Canada, Bulletin 180, 1973.

Kaufmann, Randall, *Fly Patterns of Umpqua Feather Merchants.* Glide, Oregon: Umpqua Feather Merchants, 1995.

Kaufmann, Randall, *The Fly Tiers Nymph Manual.* Portland, Oregon: Western Fisherman's Press, 1986 (2nd ed.).

Schollmeyer, Jim, *Hatch Guide For Lakes.* Portland, Oregon: Frank Amato Publications, 1995.

Schollmeyer, Jim, *Hatch Guide For The Lower Deschutes River.* Portland, Oregon: Frank Amato Publications, Inc. 1994.

Whitlock, Dave, *Guide to Aquatic Trout Foods.* New York, New York: Nick Lyons Books, 1982.



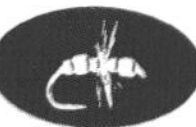

## Index

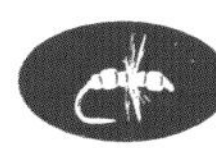